HEINEMANN MATHEMATICS 7

Textbook

These are the different types of pages and symbols used in this book:

PART ONE

This book is in four Parts. Each Part contains a number of sections relating to different areas of mathematics.

22
Handling data 1: Vertical bar graphs

These pages develop mathematical skills, concepts and facts in a wide variety of realistic contexts.

54
Extended context

Extended contexts require the use of skills from several different areas of mathematics in a section of work based on a single theme.

110
Detour: World formulae

Detours provide self-contained activities which often require an exploratory, investigative approach drawing on problem-solving skills.

 This symbol shows when you need to use a page from the accompanying workbook.

 This is a reminder of key information essential for the work of the page.

 Challenges are more-demanding activities designed to stimulate further thought and discussion.

 Investigations enhance the work of the page by providing additional opportunities to develop and use problem-solving skills.

Contents

THE HERALD

206th year   No 186   **SATURDAY 3rd AUGUST 1996**   **THIRTY-FIVE PENCE**

STAR RETIRES

LENA LAMBERT of the TV series Crown Street retired last night.

She played in the first episode in 1960 and quickly became one of the programme's best loved characters. 17 million viewers tune into the Street each week.

£2000 RAISED

Bob McCamley, 34, used to weigh 109 kg. After 3 months of diet and exercise, he now weighs 88½ kg. He lost 23 centimetres from his waistline and raised money for medical research.

1196  1996

UPLIN OCTOCENTENARY

THE TOWN celebrates 800 years. The bridge over the LIN was built in 1407.

WRANGLE OVER BABIES

"THIS IS my baby", says mother. Doctors say the week-old child was one of two babies born within 10 minutes of each other.

See page 2 for the full story.

NO CLASSES FOR 700 PUPILS

ASBESTOS safety checks were carried out at Turnbull High School in Hampton. This work resulted in a holiday on Thursday and yesterday for 700 pupils.

Test flight for new plane

The new X57 jet has just successfully completed its first test flight.

IN THE LEAD

Kay Munn, 20, was 1st in the Orinda Golf Tournament yesterday after a round of 71.

Numbers in the environment

Numbers are used in all these news stories. For example £2000 is the amount of money raised for **medical research**.

1 Look at the story above with the heading '£2000 RAISED'.
What does each of these numbers refer to?

(a) 109   **(b)** 3   **(c)** 23   **(d)** 34

2 Read the paper to find what each of these refers to.

(a) 700   **(b)** 1196   **(c)** 099 271 6033
(d) A613   **(e)** thirty-five   **(f)** X57
(g) £4·96   **(h)** octocentenary   **(i)** 1st   **(j)** 71

3 Read the paper to find, and then record,

(a) a number of restaurants
(b) a woman's age
(c) an opening time
(d) the number of years *The Herald* has been published
(e) a car model number
(f) a percentage of cotton in material
(g) a reference for ordering a T-shirt.

4 Make up your own news story with numbers in it.

1 Workbook page 24 contains 12 coupons for a 'Famous People' competition.
Each coupon has a two-digit number. Which of the numbers are

(a) odd   (b) even
(c) greater than 70   (d) less than 30?

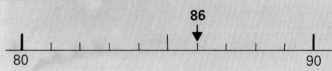

Walt Disney's number is 86.
This number is 90 **to the nearest ten**.

2 Write each coupon number to the nearest ten.
Record like this:

Walt Disney – 90

3 In the competition you win a prize if you pick the coupon
with the number **nearest to 50**.
Whose picture is on the winning coupon?

4 You win a £20 prize if you pick the number **nearest to 90**.
What do you think should happen to the prize money?

5 Which of the numbers divide exactly by   (a) 3   (b) 9   (c) 4?

6 Whose picture is on the coupon with a number which is

(a) a multiple of 5
(b) greater than 50   **and**   a multiple of 8
(c) greater than 60   **and**   a multiple of 7
(d)   odd   **and**   divisible by 9?

7 Find winning coupons for these special prizes:

Special Prize	SPECIAL PRIZE	EXTRA SPECIAL PRIZE
for the famous person whose number is **half** of one of the other numbers.	Two famous people whose numbers add to give **100**	for the famous person whose number is the same as his or her age at death.

8 (a) Cut out the 12 coupons from **Workbook page 24**.

   (b) The coupons can be put together like dominoes.
There are 3 coupons in this domino chain.
How many coupons are there in the longest domino chain that **you** can make?

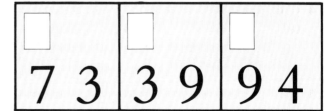

Keep your coupons for Textbook page 3.

You need the 12 'Famous People' coupons.

1 (a) Put the coupons for John Lennon and Cleopatra together
to make **one thousand eight hundred and ninety-eight.**

(b) Find the pairs of coupons needed to win these prizes:

1st prize: two thousand seven hundred and sixty-one
2nd prize: five thousand six hundred and fifty-two
3rd prize: four thousand and forty nine.

(c) You win **4th prize** with the coupons for
Anna Pavlova/John Lennon.
Write the winning number in words.

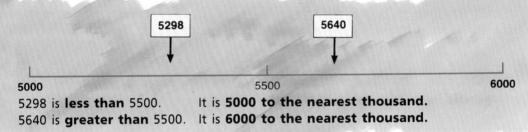

5298 is **less than** 5500.   It is **5000 to the nearest thousand.**
5640 is **greater than** 5500. It is **6000 to the nearest thousand.**

2 Put these pairs side by side. Write each number **to the nearest thousand.**

(a) Mary, Queen of Scots, and Walt Disney   `7 3 8 6`

(b) Marie Curie and Ghandi   **(c)** John Lennon and Abraham Lincoln
(d) Princess Diana and Tenzing   **(e)** Walt Disney and Henry VIII
(f) Mother Theresa and Mary, Queen of Scots
(g) Cleopatra and Marie Curie.

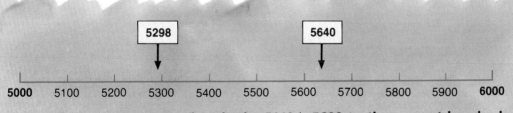

5298 is **5300 to the nearest hundred.**   5640 is **5600 to the nearest hundred.**

3 Put these coupons side by side. Write the number **to the nearest hundred**.
(a) Marie Curie/Abraham Lincoln   **(b)** Anna Pavlova/Mary, Queen of Scots
(c) Tenzing/Ghandi   **(d)** Abraham Lincoln/Mother Theresa.

4 With which pairs of coupons would you win these prizes?

(a)    **(b)**   **(c)**

PRIZE Nearest to 7300   PRIZE Nearest to 2800   PRIZE Nearest to 4000

5 Which **three** coupons do you need to win each of these prizes?

1st prize: five hundred and sixty-one thousand, eight hundred and forty-nine
2nd prize: seven hundred and thirty-two thousand, seven hundred and ninety-eight
3rd prize: three hundred and ninety-four thousand, and eighty-six.

Some pages from the Goodie catalogue are at the end of this textbook.

Look at the **Goodies** catalogue.

On **catalogue page 72** the reference for
this calculator is **EG 7219**.
The letters **EG** represent **E**lectronic **G**oods.

SUPER
CALCULATOR
Solar
powered
EG 7219
£6·60

SPECIAL OFFER

1 (a) List other pairs of letters which are used for catalogue references.
  (b) Write the words you think each pair of letters represents.

**The number part of a catalogue reference can have a meaning.
For example, 7219 is item 19 on page 72.**

2 What do these catalogue numbers mean: **(a)** 6913   **(b)** 6902   **(c)** 7221?

3 Invent catalogue numbers for these items: **(a)** item 12 on page 93
  (b) item 4 on page 26   **(c)** item 3 on page 2.

4 Use the catalogue section to check that
  FW 7103 refers to a pair of trainers.
  Now find the items which have
  these catalogue references:
  (a) SW 7121   **(b)** FW 7108
  (c) EG 7202   **(d)** SE 6905

5 What is
  this man
  buying?

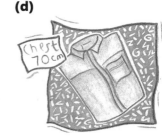

Quantity	Catalogue reference
1	FW 7101
2	EG 7221
4	EG 7210

Sometimes the size and colour can be included in the catalogue reference.
For example, **FC W 74** could stand for **F**ashion **C**lothing – **W**hite – **C**hest size **74** cm.

6 Write catalogue references for these fashion items:

(a)

Chest 76 cm

(b)

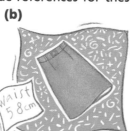

Waist 58 cm

(c)

Waist 60 cm

(d)

Chest 70 cm

The staff at Goodies each have a works number.
The number is the date when they first started working for
Goodies.

Jane Drake started working for Goodies on the
4th of September 1978. Her works number is 04 09 78.

04	09	78
day	month	year

7 Write the works numbers for

	Name	Starting date
(a)	P. McLean	26th May 1969
(b)	E. Warbrick	5th October 1984
(c)	M. Suleman	10th July 1971

8 On what date did each of these people
  join Goodies?

	Name	Works number
(a)	H. Tosaki	17 11 83
(b)	B. Saunders	08 04 80
(c)	L. Boni	30 10 78

Jane is the warehouse manager for **Goodies**.
In her job she has to work out the amount of stock in the warehouse.

She can add 376 and 94 in different ways.

On paper	Using a calculator	Mentally
376 +94	Enter 376. Press ➕ 9 4 =	376 + **4** make 380 380 + **90** make . . .

Use the five numbers on the boxes for questions 1 to 7.

1 Write as many pairs of the numbers as you can like this: 94
There are ten possible pairs. Add each pair. +376
_____

2 Find the sum of all **five** numbers.

3 Which **four** of the numbers when added give 48 766?

4 Which **three** of the numbers give a total of 4387?

5 Find the answer to 376 − 94.

6 Use the numbers to write as many different subtractions of a smaller number from a larger number as you can. Find each answer.

7 Start with the largest number. Subtract each other number in turn like this:

Enter 48291. Press ➖ 9 4 ➖ 3 7 6 ➖ 5 ➖ 3 9 1 7 =

Write the answer.

These boxes in the **Goodies** warehouse contain cassettes. The number of cassettes left in each box is shown on the star.

429	62	57
938	216	1231
82	189	1187
764	78	43

8 How many cassettes are there altogether for  *Shooting Stars a collection*

The Movers Greatest Hits

Top Rap

Number 1 Hits

90s Solid Gold

9 How many cassettes have to be ordered to make up a stock of 2000 for each?

10 Do Workbook page 2.

Use the prices on page 73 of the Goodies catalogue.

1 Find the cost of
    (a) 5 gold name pendants   **(b)** 15 GIANT packs of stickers
    (c) 8 small badges   **(d)** 34 albums for stickers
    (e) 6 rulers (25 cm)   **(f)** 18 large T-shirts.

2 Copy each of these special notices for bedroom doors.
    Find the cost of each when printed in gold, silver and black.

(a)   **(b)**   **(c)**

A GENIUS SLEEPS HERE

DANGER
Stray parents will be shot

HEADQUARTERS
MESSY BEDROOM SOCIETY

3 Sharon wanted to buy a notice for her brother.
    Which of these would be cheapest?

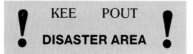
! KEE POUT !
DISASTER AREA

BEWARE
SWEATY SOCKS KEPT HERE

NO GO AREA
Enter at your peril

(a) in gold letters   **(b)** in silver letters   **(c)** in black letters

4 Make up a special notice, costing
less than £2, for your own door.
Give the catalogue reference,
colour of print, and cost.

5 Find the cost of 100 of each of these:
    (a) large T-shirts   **(b)** sets of large posters on SPECIAL OFFER
    (c) silver name pendants   **(d)** large badges   **(e)** toothbrushes.

6 How many stickers are there in
    (a) 120 small packets   **(b)** 275 small packets   **(c)** 438 small packets
    (d) 10 SUPERGIANT packs   **(e)** 9 SUPERGIANT packs   **(f)** 6 SUPERGIANT packs?

7 (a) Will 75 small packets of stickers fill an album?
    (b) Will 10 GIANT packs fill 2 albums?
    (c) Will 5 SUPERGIANT packs fill 3 albums?
    (d) John has 200 full albums. Is he a sticker millionaire?

8 What is the item in each of these orders? Find each total cost.

	Quantity	Catalogue reference		Quantity	Catalogue reference
(a)	80	PG 399	**(c)**	200	PG 432
(b)	185	PG 433	**(d)**	270	PG 400

Watch this T-shirt!

7

Whole
numbers 1:
Multiplication
by tens and
units

Use the prices on page 73 of the Goodies catalogue.

Here are two ways of finding the cost of 28 small packets of stickers.

Using a calculator

Enter **28.**

Press **✕** **3** **2** **=** to give **896.**

The total cost is £8·96.

On paper

```
  32p
× 28
 256
 640
896p
```

1 Find the cost of

    (a) 19 small packets of stickers   **(b)** 25 small badges   **(c)** 17 gold name pendants
    (d) 34 silver name pendants   **(e)** 27 toothbrushes   **(f)** 30 large badges.

2 Find the cost of each of these T-shirt messages:

  (a)   **(b)**   **(c)**

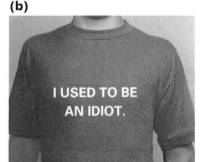
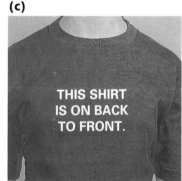

WATCH THIS SPACE

I USED TO BE AN IDIOT.

THIS SHIRT IS ON BACK TO FRONT.

3 Make up a message for a T-shirt.
   Write a note to your mum to ask her to order it for you.
   Give details of size, colour, message, catalogue reference and cost.

4 Your class decides to buy items **with your school name printed on them.**
   Use Order Form 1 on **Workbook page 3** to copy and complete the form below.
   Order enough items for everyone in your class.

Your school name

Quantity	Catalogue reference	Description	Cost of one	Total cost
	PG 407	Large badge printed " "		
	PG 496			
	PG 494			

5 How much would it cost to give every pupil in your school a
   small badge with the school name on it?

6 Learnwell School wanted to order large T-shirts with the school
   name on them. They decided to use one of these names.

Challenge

   LEARNWELL   LEARNWELL   LEARNWELL   LEARNWELL
SECONDARY SCHOOL   SECONDARY   SCHOOL

Each T-shirt, with name, cost £5·95. What name and size of print did they choose?

Notices and computer numbers

Use the prices on page 73 of the Goodies catalogue.

A special notice in black letters cost £1·54. How many letters does it have?
You can find how many times 7p is contained in 154p in several ways.

On paper

$$7 \overline{\smash{)}\,154} = 22$$

Using a calculator

Enter **154.** Press ÷ 7 = to give **22.**

Mentally Thinks

There are 22 letters on the notice.

1 How many letters are there on these notices?

	(a)	(b)	(c)	(d)	(e)	(f)
Colour of print	black	black	silver	gold	black	gold
Total cost	63p	84p	99p	£2	£2·03	£3·20

2 Look at Order Form 2 on **Workbook page 3**. Some information is missing.
The number of sets of posters can be found by dividing £45 by £5.
Nine sets were bought. Complete Order Form 2.

Quantity	Catalogue reference	Description	Cost of one	Total cost
9	PG 399	Set of 6 small posters	£ 5	£ 45
	PG 499		£ 8	£ 136

3 Elizabeth ordered one of these items
with her name on it. Steve and
Winston also ordered one item.
Find out what each of them bought.

1	PG 494	78p
1	PG 497	41p
1	PG 495	£1·45

4 The costs of special notices for bedroom doors are given below.
How many letters are on each notice and what colours are they?

(a) 81p **(b)** £1 **(c)** £2·43 **(d)** £2·45

The **Goodies** computer puts an extra digit
(never zero) on the catalogue number.
This is so that the **computer number**
always divides exactly by 9.

Silver name pendant: Catalogue reference **PG 385**

The number will divide exactly by 9
if an extra 2 is put at the end.
The computer number is **PG 3852**.

$$9 \overline{\smash{)}\,3\,8^{2}5^{7}2} = 428$$

Seventy-what
divides exactly
by 9?

Challenge

5 Find the computer numbers for **(a)** a small red T-shirt **(b)** a door name plate
(c) a Tiger poster **(d)** a pack of pencils.

Ask your teacher what to do next.

Multiples

1 The multiples of 2 are 2, 4, 6, . . .

The multiples of 2 have been shaded on this number grid.

The numbers in the grid are arranged in a spiral.

73	74	75	76	77	78	79	80	81	82
72	43	44	45	46	47	48	49	50	83
71	42	21	22	23	24	25	26	51	84
70	41	20	7	8	9	10	27	52	85
69	40	19	6	1	2	11	28	53	86
68	39	18	5	4	3	12	29	54	87
67	38	17	16	15	14	13	30	55	88
66	37	36	35	34	33	32	31	56	89
65	64	63	62	61	60	59	58	57	90
100	99	98	97	96	95	94	93	92	91

Go to Workbook page 15.

Factors

> 16 can be divided exactly by 1.   1 is a factor of 16.
> 16 can be divided exactly by 2.   2 is a factor of 16.
> 16 **cannot** be divided exactly by 3.   3 is **not** a factor of 16.

2 List all the factors of 16.

3 Which of these numbers are factors of 15?   ① ⑦

4 Find all the factors of these numbers:
  (a) 6   **(b)** 8   **(c)** 14   **(d)** 9   **(e)** 32   **(f)** 5

5 Area of rectangle **A** = 2×6 = 12 cm²
2,6 is a **factor pair** of 12.

Area of rectangle **B** = 1×12 = 12 cm²
1,12 is a **factor pair** of 12.

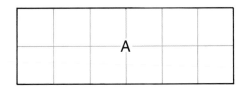

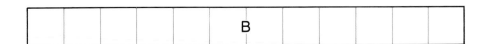

On centimetre-squared paper draw a different rectangle with an area of 12 cm² and use it to find another factor pair of 12.

6 Draw rectangles to find all the factor pairs of
  (a) 8   **(b)** 15   **(c)** 18

7 Without drawing rectangles, find all the factor pairs of
  (a) 6   **(b)** 10   **(c)** 35   **(d)** 4   **(e)** 28   **(f)** 17   **(g)** 24

Ask your teacher what to do next.

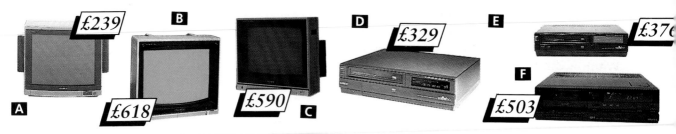

Sarah wants to buy a TV set and a video recorder. She decides to 'shop' around.

A £239
B
C £590
D £329
E £376
F £503
£618

1 Write the cost of each of **A** to **F** **to the nearest hundred** pounds.

Sarah calculated **mentally** the approximate cost of 3 different choices.

Items A and E

239 is about **2** hundred
376 is about **4** hundred.
2 hundred and **4** hundred
is **6** hundred.

The cost is about **£600**.

Items B and D

6 hundred and
3 hundred is
9 hundred.

The cost is about **£900**.

Items C and F

6 hundred and
5 hundred is
11 hundred.

The cost is about **£1100**.

2 Calculate **mentally** the approximate cost of

(a) **B** and **F**   (b) **C** and **D**   (c) **C** and **E**   (d) **A** and **D**.

3 Use a calculator to find exact costs for question **2**.
Compare them with your estimates.

G £780

4 Sarah also wanted to buy this music system.
Calculate **mentally** the rough cost of items

(a) **B, D,** and **G**
(b) **C, F,** and **G**.

Check your estimates with a calculator.

Sarah likes playing computer games with friends.
She estimated her score **in thousands** for this computer game.

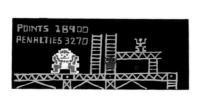

POINTS 18900
PENALTIES 3270

18 900 is about **19** thousand
Take away **3** thousand
My score is about **16** thousand

5 Find her **exact** score using a calculator.

6 (a) Estimate the score in thousands for each of Sarah's friends below.
(b) Find the exact score and compare it with your estimate.

Joanne POINTS 9600 PENALTIES 1790

Melanie POINTS 24200 PENALTIES 6850

Kevin POINTS 17200 PENALTIES 4190

7 Make estimates of these scores.
Does either beat Melanie's score?

Stuart	Points 21 900	Penalties 8050
Shaheen	Points 18 100	Penalties 2890

Do all the calculations on this page mentally.

1 Darren, Mike and Jane are buying some sweets.
They choose three items costing 6p, 28p and 4p each.
They each find the total in a different way.
Which is the easiest order and why?

2 Make cards like these:

2 3 4 6 7 8

(a) Shuffle all six cards and lay out **five** in a row
Place in pairs cards which total ten.
Find the sum of the five numbers.

(b) Do this two more times.

3 Change the cards **6 7 8** by adding ten to each to give **16 17 18**.

Find the sum of each pair: **(a)** **16 4** **(b)** **17 3** **(c)** **18 2**

4 Shuffle all six cards. Lay out **five** of them. Find their sum.
Do this two more times.

5 Change the cards **4 3 2** by adding ten to each to give **14 13 12**.

Find the sum of each pair: **(a)** **16 14** **(b)** **17 13** **(c)** **18 12**

6 Shuffle all six cards. Lay out **five** of them. Find their sum.
Do this two more times.

You can add $17 + 28 + 13 + 5 + 2$ by looking for pairs.

30   30   The total is **$30 + 30 + 5 = 65$**.

7 Find the sum of
(a) $5 + 18 + 5 + 12$ (b) $17 + 23 + 15 + 5$ (c) $26 + 17 + 15 + 5 + 14$

8 (a) Multiply 7, 5 and 2 in three different orders like this:
$7 \times 5 \times 2$ $5 \times 2 \times 7$ $7 \times 2 \times 5$
(b) Which is the easiest order and why?

9 Multiply in the easiest order:
(a) $8 \times 10 \times 4$ (b) $100 \times 7 \times 6$ (c) $9 \times 2 \times 7$ (d) $6 \times 20 \times 9$

10 Investigate **(a)** $16 - 4 - 2$ **(b)** $16 \div 4 \div 2$.
Explain why the pair of numbers you take first is important.

Ask your teacher what to do next.

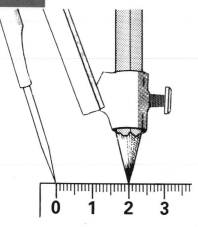

The **radius** of a circle is the distance from **centre** to **circumference**.

The diagrams show how to set compasses and draw a circle of radius 2 cm.

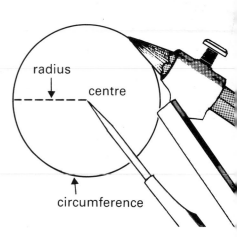

Use compasses to make these designs.

1 Bull's-eye

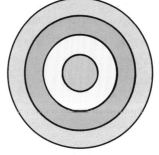

- Draw a circle with radius 8 cm.
- **Use the same centre** and draw circles with radius 6 cm, 4 cm and 2 cm to make a bull's-eye design.
- Colour your design.

2 Dartboard

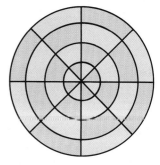

- Draw another bull's-eye as you did in question **1**.
- Draw lines through the centre as shown to make a dartboard design.
- Colour your design.

3 Circles and lines

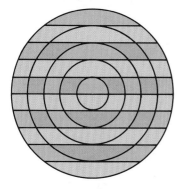

- Make a bull's-eye design and draw straight lines as shown.
- Colour your design.

4 Pond ripples

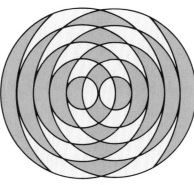

- Make this pond ripples design by drawing two intersecting bull's-eyes **with centres 4 cm apart.**
- Colour your design.

5 Make a wall display of your designs.

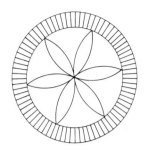

1 You can draw this design on a paper plate using compasses.

Try the design first on plain paper.

(a) Set your compasses at 5 cm and leave them set.

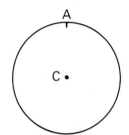

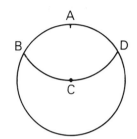

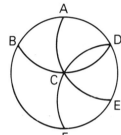

(b) Draw a circle and mark a point **A** on the circumference.

(c) Use point **A** as a new centre and draw part of a circle, **BCD**.

(d) With new centre **D**, draw another part circle, **ACE**.
With new centre **E**, draw another part circle, **DCF**.

(e) Go on like this until you have a design with six 'petals'.

You need a white paper plate.
2 Decide how to find the 'centre' of the plate and what radius you should use to make a design like the one at the top of the page.

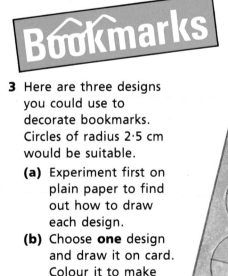

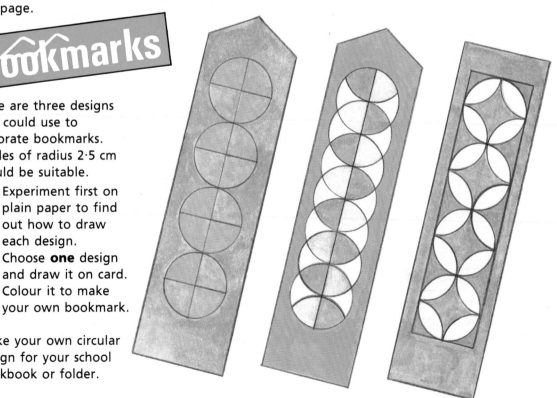

3 Here are three designs you could use to decorate bookmarks. Circles of radius 2·5 cm would be suitable.

(a) Experiment first on plain paper to find out how to draw each design.

(b) Choose **one** design and draw it on card. Colour it to make your own bookmark.

4 Make your own circular design for your school workbook or folder.

Ask your teacher what to do next.

1 Write in decimal form:

    (a) 2 tenths   **(b)** 7 tenths   **(c)** 1 unit and 3 tenths   **(d)** 18 tenths   **(e)** 30 tenths

2 Write in decimal form: **(a)** $\frac{7}{10}$ **(b)** $2\frac{6}{10}$ **(c)** $\frac{19}{10}$ **(d)** $\frac{1}{2}$ **(e)** $4\frac{1}{5}$

This plan is drawn to a scale of **1 cm to 0·1 km**.

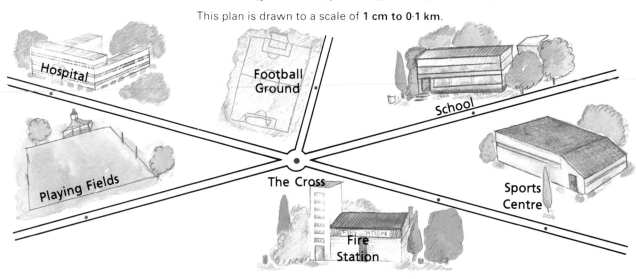

3 Measure the lengths between the red dots along the roads.
   How far is it, in **kilometres**, by road from

    (a) the cross to the playing fields   **(b)** the fire station to the hospital
    (c) the school to the playing fields   **(d)** the football ground to the hospital
    (e) the fire station to the school   **(f)** the sports centre to the football ground?

4 Four boys ran a race of 100 m.

   Gary ran the race in 11·7 seconds.
   Steve was 2 tenths of a second slower than Gary.
   Tom was 4 tenths of a second slower than Gary.
   Waseem was 5 tenths of a second faster than Tom.

    (a) Who won the race?
    (b) How long did the last boy take?

35·5 cm

49·6 cm

5 (a) Find the total length in centimetres of the frame.
    (b) Picture framing is sold in $\frac{1}{2}$ m, 1 m, $1\frac{1}{2}$ m, and 2 m lengths.
       What length of framing must be bought for this picture?
    (c) What length of framing is left over?

6 The table shows the points for three dives in a competition.

    (a) Find the total points for each diver.
    (b) Name the winner and the runner up.
    (c) What is the difference between their total points?

	Jane	Tracy	Kelly
Dive 1	69·4	70·0	66·4
Dive 2	72·8	55·9	78·3
Dive 3	58·3	64·2	58·4

1 What decimal fraction
of this pattern is
coloured
  (a) red
  (b) yellow
  (c) blue?

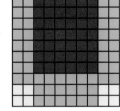

2 Arrow **A** points to 2·59 on this scale.
Write in decimal form the numbers
shown by the other arrows.

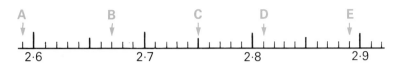

3 Write each of these in decimal form:
  (a) 37 hundredths   **(b)** 9 hundredths   **(c)** 2 tenths and 5 hundredths
  (d) 5 units and 4 hundredths   **(e)** 1 unit, 4 tenths and 8 hundredths.

4 Write each number with a decimal point so that
the 4 has a value of 4 hundredths:
  (a) 134   **(b)** 74   **(c)** 6594   **(d)** 14   **(e)** 304   **(f)** 4

5 Write each of these in decimal form: **(a)** $\frac{6}{100}$ **(b)** $1\frac{3}{100}$ **(c)** $\frac{3}{4}$ **(d)** $2\frac{1}{4}$

6 Write the following lengths in centimetres, or metres and centimetres:
  (a) 0·71 m   **(b)** 7·60 m   **(c)** 0·05 m   **(d)** 1·76 m   **(e)** 20·04 m   **(f)** 0·8 m

178 cm

4 m 6 cm

98 cm

285 cm

3 m 40 cm

7 Write the heights shown above, in **metres**, in decimal form.

8 The times taken, in seconds, by six swimmers in a race were

  52·08   52·41   51·65   52·90   52·29   51·77

Write these times in order from fastest to slowest.

9 This is what a TV commentator said about
the first four in a 200 m race:

...Lorna is 7 hundredths of a second behind the winner...

...and a tired Eileen finishes in 3 hundredths over 24 seconds...

...Anya finishes 6 hundredths outside the championship record...

...Kathy has broken the championship record...

Championship Record 23·34

Winner's time 23·29

  (a) Make a list from 1st to 4th of the athletes and their times.
  (b) By how many hundredths of a second did the winner break the record?

Use the prices on page 69 of the Goodies catalogue.

Here are two ways of finding the total cost of
a football (£13·35) and a table tennis set (£17·85).

Using a calculator

Enter £13·35 as   **13.35**

Press **+ 1 7 . 8 5 =**

to give   **31.2**

On paper

£13·35
+£17·85
————
£31·20

The total cost is **£31·20**

1 If you ignore any special offer, what is the total cost of
  (a) a tennis set and a badminton set   **(b)** a bicycle helmet and a lighting set
  (c) booted skates and ice skates   **(d)** a rugby ball and a twistball?

2 Which of the pairs of items in question **1** are on special offer for cash?
Find the special offer cost in each case.

3 How much do you save when you buy the bicycle, helmet
and lighting set, using the gold star offer?

4 Find the total cost of the items listed in each of these Order Forms.

(a)

Quantity	Catalogue reference	Price
1	SE 6902	
1	SE 6947	
1	SE 6901	

(b)

Quantity	Catalogue reference	Price
1	SE 6935	
1	SE 6948	
1	SE 6912	

5 Check each order to find if a special offer applies. If so, find the new total cost.

For questions 6, 7, 8 and 10 use the Order Forms on Workbook pages 3 and 4.

6 Dave ordered two items from **page 69 of the Goodies catalogue**.
Complete Order Form 3. How much did he pay altogether?

7 Carewell Hospital spent exactly £70 on three different sports items.
Complete Order Form 4. What was the third item ordered?

Quantity	Catalogue reference
1	SE 6935
1	SE 6948
1	SE 6912

8 You have £100 to spend on sports equipment.
  (a) Choose items and complete Order Form 5.
  Remember the special offers.
  (b) How much is left after you pay for the goods?

9 The items listed in the order form
above were paid for in 20 weekly
payments.
What was the **total** weekly payment?

10 You can spend up to £4·50 per week.
Choose goods from **page 69 of the
Goodies catalogue**.
Complete Order Form 6.

1 Lucy recovers chairs and makes cushions. Copy and complete her calculations to find the length of material needed

(a) to make 3 cushions
(b) to recover 7 chairs
(c) to recover 5 bedsettees.

2 Alex needs 5·8 m of material to make one duvet cover. How many metres will he need to make

(a) 2   (b) 6   (c) 9 duvet covers?

3 How much altogether did Donna pay for

4 m of jersey at £2·01 per metre
5 m of acrylic at £3·05 per metre and
6 m of velvet at £16·75 per metre?

WANTED: SALES ASSISTANT FOR FABRIC SHOP
WAGE: 346.5p PER HOUR

4 How much will Michael earn as sales assistant in

(a) a working day of 8 hours
(b) 5 working days?

VACANCY: SALES MANAGER FOR FABRIC SHOP
WAGE: £43.67 PER DAY

5 How much will Julie earn as sales manager in

(a) a working week of 5 days
(b) 4 working weeks?

6 Syeda ordered 12 m of velour to make 3 pairs of curtains. Each curtain uses 1·85 m of velour. What length of velour

(a) did she use altogether   (b) was left over?

> To multiply by **10**,
> move each digit **one** place to the left. $10 \times 3·85 = 38·5$
>
> To multiply by **100**,
> move each digit **two** places to the left. $100 \times 3·8 = 380$

7 'Simply Tweeds' makes clothing from tweed.
One suit uses 3·4 m of tweed and one coat uses 2·5 m of tweed.
Find the length of tweed needed for

(a) 10 suits   (b) 100 suits   (c) 10 coats   (d) 100 coats.

8 For each type of material on special offer, find the cost of   (a) 10 metres   (b) 100 metres.

SPECIAL OFFER
Nylon   £1.08 per metre
Felt   £2.63 per metre
Corduroy   £3.65 per metre

9 Erica makes curtains. She uses 12·4 m of material for a pair of curtains.
How many metres will she need for

(a) 10 pairs   (b) 100 pairs?

You need a calculator.

4×3.46	45×3.46	452×3.46
Enter **3.46**	Enter **3.46**	Enter **3.46**
Press ✕ 4 =	Press ✕ 4 5 =	Press ✕ 4 5 2 =
The answer is **13.84**	The answer is **155.7**	The answer is **1563.92**

1 Write the answers to:

   (a) 54×3.8 **(b)** 17×1.2 **(c)** 30×18.6 **(d)** 3×17.8
   (e) 20×13.94 **(f)** 327×12.87 **(g)** 468×23.91 **(h)** 427×2.5

2 Goodies hire 14 vans to deliver the catalogue goods.
   The cost of hiring one van is £12·55 per day.
   Find the cost of hiring

   (a) one van for a year   **(b)** all the vans for a year.

3 Each van uses an average of 83·6 litres of petrol per week.
   How many litres of petrol does a van use in one year?

4 Petrol costs 42·5p per litre. Calculate to the nearest penny the
   petrol bill for   **(a)** one van per year   **(b)** all 14 vans per year?

Use the prices on pages 69 and 72 of the Goodies catalogue.

The football costs £13·35. When paid over 20 weeks at 67p per week what is the
extra cost?

To find the total cost:

Enter 67p as **0.67**

Press ✕ 2 0 = to give **13.4**

FOOTBALL
SE 6901
£13·35
20 weeks
at 67p

The total cost over 20 weeks is £13·40. The **extra cost** is 5p.

5 Find the **extra cost**, if any, when you pay for these items over 20 weeks:
   (a) the lighting set   **(b)** the rugby ball   **(c)** the video-recorder.

6 You can pay for the bicycle in 20, 38 or 50 weekly payments.
   Find the extra cost, if any, when you pay in each of these three ways.

Ali's Payment Card

Week 1	£1·06	paid
Week 2	£1·06	paid
Week 3	£1·06	paid

7 Ali has paid 22 weekly payments of £1·06 for a snooker table.
   (a) How much has he paid?
   (b) How much more has he still to pay?

Ask your teacher what to do next.

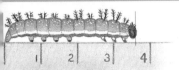

The length of the caterpillar is between 3 cm and 4 cm.

This ruler is marked in **centimetres** and **millimetres**. The length is **3 cm 6 mm**.

This ruler is marked in **millimetres**. The length of the caterpillar is **36 mm**.

1 How many **millimetres** equal 1 centimetre? Copy and complete: 1 cm = ☐ mm.

2 Change to **millimetres**:

(a) 20 cm (b) 6 cm 4 mm (c) 12 cm 1 mm (d) $3\frac{1}{2}$ cm

3 Measure the length in **millimetres** of each of these caterpillars.

A   B   C

D   E

One millimetre is one tenth of a centimetre. This can be written **1 mm = 0·1 cm**
The length of caterpillar **A** can be written as **42 mm** or **4 cm 2 mm** or **4·2 cm**

4 (a) Measure the wingspans of these six butterflies.
Record like this: Purple Emperor 6·8 cm

Peacock

Speckled Wood

Purple
Emperor

Red Admiral

Small
Copper

Northern
Brown

(b) Which butterflies have wingspans between 35 mm and 55 mm?
(c) Find the **average** wingspan in mm of all six butterflies.
(d) The wingspan of the Purple Emperor is
6·8 cm. This is 7 cm **to the nearest cm**.
Write each of the other wingspans to the nearest cm.

This type of butterfly lives in Malaysia. It is so large that it has been drawn to scale here. **The scale is 1 cm to 2 cm.**

True wingspan $= 8.3 \times 2$ cm

$= 16.6$ cm approximately

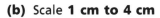

8·3 cm

1 Find the true wingspan of each butterfly below.

(a) Scale **1 cm to 3 cm**   **(b)** Scale **1 cm to 4 cm**

Swan

Scale:
1 cm to 16 cm

2 These three birds are drawn to scale.

(a) Find the approximate true wingspan in **centimetres** of each bird.

(b) List the birds in order, giving their wingspans in **metres**.

Scale:
1 cm to 25 cm

Golden Eagle

Albatross   Scale: **1 cm to 40 cm**

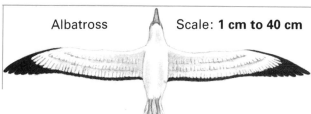

3 About what length in **metres** are the true wingspans of the Boeing 747 and the Shuttle?

Space Shuttle

Scale:
1 cm to 5 m

Boeing 747   Scale:
1 cm to 10 m

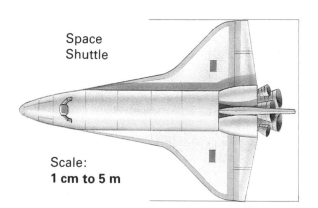
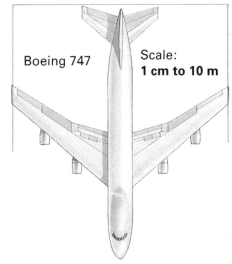

Kwickcarry Removals need new accommodation. They hire an architect, Ann Simpson, to help them find a new site.

Ann makes a rough sketch of each bulding before making an accurate scale drawing.

Rough sketch

2 m 2 m
Offices 4 m
2 m
6 m

Scale **1 cm to 2 m**

2 m is represented by 1 cm
6 m is represented by $6 \div 2 = 3$ cm
4 m is represented by $4 \div 2 = 2$ cm

Scale drawing

Offices

Use centimetre squared paper.

1 Make accurate scale drawings for **Warehouse 1** using these scales: **(a) 1 cm to 2 m**
  (b) 1 cm to 4 m **(c) 1 cm to 1 m**.

2 Make **two** accurate scale drawings for **each** of the rough sketches below.
Use scales of **1 cm to 3 m** and **1 cm to 6 m**.

Rough sketch

8 m   Warehouse 1
12 m

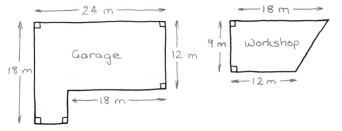

24 m
Garage   12 m
18 m
18 m

18 m
9 m   Workshop
12 m

12 m
3 m
6 m
12 m
Warehouse 2   9 m
3 m
36 m

3 A rectangular piece of land measuring 30 m by 18 m is to be made into a car park holding as many cars as possible without blocking any in. Make a rough sketch and then an accurate scale drawing of the car park, where:
  • each parking place is a 6 m by 3 m rectangle
  • the entrance and roadways are at least 9 m wide.

Challenge

Ask your teacher what to do next.

A group of pupils at Derwent School carried out a survey to find where they all went for their summer holidays.

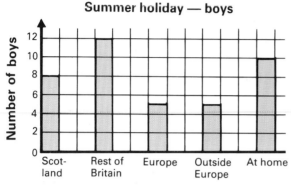

Summer holiday — boys

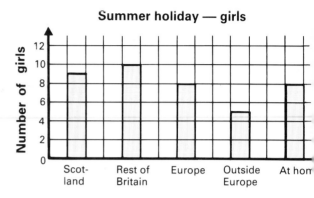

Summer holiday — girls

1 (a) For each place on the graph give the number of **boys** who had their holiday there.

(b) How many boys are there altogether in the school?

(c) What fraction of the boys stayed at home?

2 Repeat question **1** for the girls' graph.

3 What fraction of **all** the pupils had their holiday outside Europe?

All the information in both graphs above can be shown in a single graph like **P** or **Q**.

P

Summer holiday — boys and girls

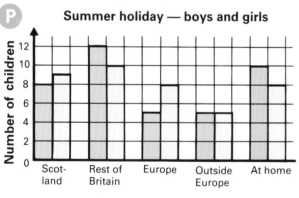

Q

Summer holiday — boys and girls

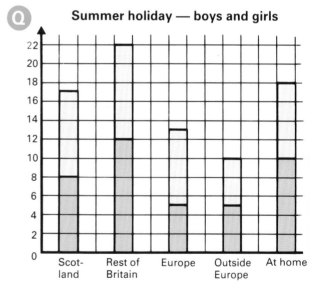

4 Where did

(a) the greatest

(b) the smallest number of pupils have their holiday?

Which graph, **P** or **Q**, shows this more clearly?

5 Where did

(a) more boys than girls have their holiday

(b) more girls than boys have their holiday?

Which graph, **P** or **Q**, shows this more clearly?

6 Collect information about your classmates' summer holidays. Use the information to draw graphs like **P** and **Q**.

The ferry company **Seaswift** keeps records of the vehicles it carries. These graphs show the vehicles carried by a **Seaswift** ferry on four crossings.

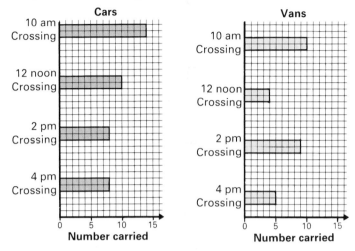

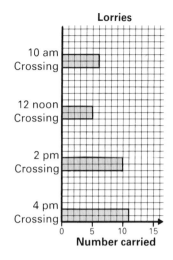

1 (a) How many cars were carried on each crossing?

(b) What was the **average** number of cars carried per crossing?

2 Repeat question **1** for vans and for lorries.

All the information in the three graphs above can be shown in a single graph like **Y** or **Z**.

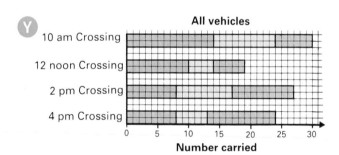

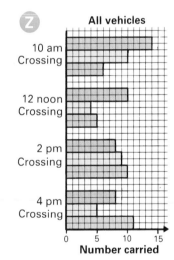

3 On which crossing was

(a) the greatest

(b) the smallest number of vehicles carried?

Which graph, **Y** or **Z**, shows this more clearly?

4 On which crossings were

(a) more

(b) fewer cars than vans carried?

Which graph, **Y** or **Z**, shows this more clearly?

5 Find the **average** number of vehicles carried per crossing.

6 Collect information about the cars, vans and lorries passing your school during the same period each day for five days. Draw your own graphs like **Y** and **Z**.

How we travel

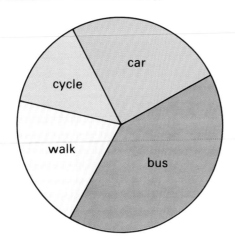

1 This is a **pie chart** showing how the pupils in one class travel to school. Which way of travelling is used by
   (a) most pupils   **(b)** fewest pupils?

2 Write **true** or **false** for each of these:
   (a) More pupils walk than cycle.
   (b) More pupils walk than travel by car.
   (c) More than half the class travel by bus.
   (d) More than half the class travel either by bus or by car.

3 About what fraction of the class
   (a) travel by car   **(b)** cycle?

4 This pie chart shows the favourite school subject chosen by some pupils. Which subject was chosen by
   (a) most pupils   **(b)** fewest pupils?

5 Into how many **equal** parts has the circle been divided?

6 There were ten pupils altogether. How many chose as their favourite subject
   (a) Art   **(b)** Mathematics   **(c)** PE?

What we like best

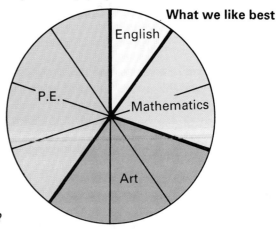

Helen's day

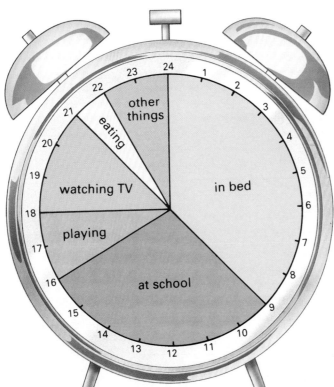

7 This pie chart shows how Helen spent one complete day. How many hours did she spend
   (a) eating
   (b) watching TV
   (c) in bed?

8 What fraction of the day did she spend
   (a) eating
   (b) watching TV
   (c) in bed?

9 Which **three** activities together took up exactly half the day?

10 Which **two** activities together took up exactly half the day?

11 **Go to Workbook page 7.**

Lisa, Rashmi, Dean and Mark played a round of crazy golf.
Their scores for each hole are shown on the scorecard.

Scorecard																			
Name	1	2	3	4	5	6	7	8	9	10	11	12	13	14	15	16	17	18	Total
Lisa	2	3	4	4	2	3	1	4	3	2	4	2	3	2	5	3	5	2	54
Rashmi	5	2	3	4	3	5	4	1	3	3	4	2	6	4	2	5	3	4	
Dean	3	3	3	1	4	2	4	3	2	5	3	3	3	3	4	3	2	3	
Mark	3	2	1	3	3	3	2	2	4	3	2	1	3	3	2	2	3	3	

1 Who had the lowest score at **(a)** hole 6 **(b)** hole 11 **(c)** hole 18?

2 At which hole did Rashmi have **(a)** her lowest score **(b)** her highest score?

3 At which hole did three players have the same score?

Lisa's lowest score was 1 and her highest score 5.
Lisa's scores ranged from 1 to 5.
The range of Lisa's scores is 5 – 1 = 4.

4 What is the range of
(a) Rashmi's scores **(b)** Mark's scores?

5 Lisa's total score for the eighteen holes was 54.
Find **mentally** the total score for
(a) Rashmi **(b)** Dean **(c)** Mark.
Check each answer **using a calculator**.

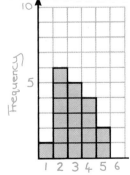

To find her **mean** (average) score for each hole, Lisa divided her total score by 18.

Enter **54.** Press **÷ 1 8 =** to give **3.**

Lisa's mean score for each hole was 3.

6 Find the mean score for each hole for
(a) Rashmi **(b)** Dean **(c)** Mark.

7 Lisa made a frequency table to find how many times she scored a 1, 2, 3, 4, 5 or 6. She then drew a graph.

Score	Tally marks	Frequency
1	I	1
2	⊞ I	6
3	⊞	5
4	IIII	4
5	II	2
6		–

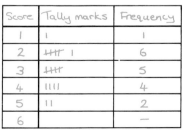

Lisa's Scores

8 Do Workbook page 8.
(You will need the crazy golf scores for Rashmi, Dean and Mark.)

The graph shows the lengths of some pupils' feet.

1 How many pupils have a foot length of
   (a) 25 cm   **(b)** 21 cm?

2 (a) Which foot length is the most common?
   (b) How many pupils have this foot length?

3 How many pupils have a foot length
   (a) greater than 23 cm
   (b) less than 23 cm?

4 How many pupils are there altogether?

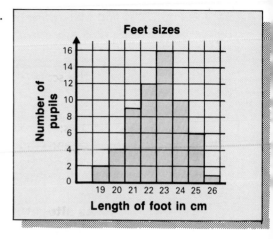

Some other pupils
measured their headband
size (head **circumference**)
to the nearest centimetre.
The table shows their results.

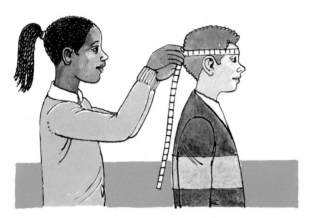

Circumference of head in cm	Tally marks	Number of pupils
51	II	2
52	ⅢⅠ	5
53	ⅢⅠ ⅢⅠ IIII	14
54	ⅢⅠ ⅢⅠ ⅢⅠ III	18
55	ⅢⅠ ⅢⅠ ⅢⅠ	15
56	ⅢⅠ ⅢⅠ	10
57	ⅢⅠ II	7
58	I	1

5 Use the information in the table to
   draw a bar graph on squared paper.
   Label each axis as shown.

6 (a) How many pupils altogether had
      their head measured?
   (b) Which head circumference is the
      most common?
   (c) How many pupils have this head
      circumference?
   (d) What fraction of the total number
      of pupils have this head
      circumference?

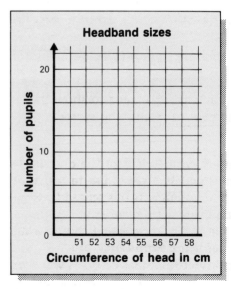

7 Make a table like the one shown above. Collect the
   headband sizes, measured to the nearest centimetre, of
   the pupils in your year group.
   Draw a bar graph of your results.

Work with a partner.

1 You need two dice.

The difference between the scores on these two dice is 4 − 1 = 3.

(a) Make a table like this:
(b) Throw the two dice and find the difference between the scores. Put a tally mark in the table to record your answer.
   Do this 100 times altogether.
   Your partner should keep a count of how many times you throw the dice.

Difference	Tally marks	Frequency (Number of times)
0		
1		
2		
3		
4		
5		

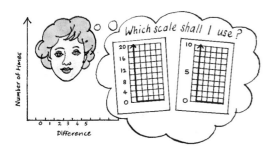

(c) Draw a graph of your results. Label each axis and choose a suitable scale for the **Frequency (Number of times) axis.**
(d) Which difference occurred most often? Compare this with others in your class.

2 You need a newspaper containing football results.

Arsenal	1
Crystal Palace	1
Leeds United	0
Liverpool	3
Manchester City	2
Nottingham Forest	2
Aston Villa	1
Tottenham Hotspur	0

A table can be made to show the number of teams who scored 0, 1, 2, 3, . . . goals.

(a) Make a table like the one shown.
(b) **For 100 teams**, use tally marks to record how many teams scored 0, 1, 2, 3, . . . goals.
(c) Draw a graph of your results. Label each axis and choose a suitable scale for the **Frequency** axis.
(d) Which number of goals was scored most often? Compare your result with others in your class.

Goals scored	Tally marks	Number of teams
0	II	
1	III	
2	II	
3	I	
4		

Ask your teacher what to do next.

1 The numbers in the red boxes are found by multiplying the numbers in the **columns**.

The numbers in the blue boxes are found by multiplying the numbers in the **rows**.

$2 \times 5 \rightarrow$

10	12	$\leftarrow 3 \times 4$
2	3
5	4

	10	12
$2 \times 3 \rightarrow$ 6	2	3
$5 \times 4 \rightarrow$ 20	5	4

Now copy and complete these grids.

(a)

	6	15
10		
9		

(b)

	21	24
28		
18		

(c)

	36	48
54		
32		

(d)

	56	66
48		
77		

(e)

	48	65
52		
60		

Use a calculator for questions 2 and 3.

2 Copy and complete:
  (a) $73 \times \boxed{}6 = 4088$
  (b) $8\boxed{} \times \boxed{}7 = 4042$
  (c) $1081 \div \boxed{}7 = 23$
  (d) $646 \div \boxed{}\boxed{} = 19$

3 Peter posted two sizes of parcel. One size cost 42p and the other 54p. Twelve parcels cost him £5·64. How many of each size did he post?

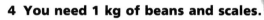

4 You need 1 kg of beans and scales.
  (a) Guess the approximate number of beans in 1 kg.
  (b) Check your guess without counting **all** the beans.
  Write about how you did this.

Challenge

5 (a) Colour this shape on 2 cm squared paper and cut it out.
  (b) Make two **equal** straight cuts across the shape and fit the three pieces together to form a **square**. The dotted line shows the first cut.

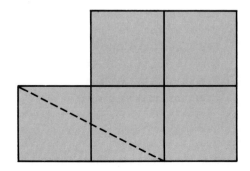

1 For a snack you may choose one item
from the DRINKS mug and one item
from the EATS jar.

(a) Which two items would **you**
choose?

(b) Make a list of all the different
possible ways of choosing two
items. Your list could begin like
this: juice and bun

2 At activity time you may choose one
indoor and one outdoor activity.

(a) Which two activities would **you**
choose?

(b) List all the different possible ways
of choosing two activities.

3 **Do Workbook page 9.**

4 **You need squared paper.**
At lunch time you may have a three-
course meal by choosing one item from
each part of the menu.

(a) Which three-course meal would
you choose?

(b) Use squared paper to make a table
to show all the different possible
three-course meals.
How many are there altogether?

(c) Two new items are added to the
menu – melon in the first course
and cheese in the third course.
How many different three-course
meals are now possible?

5 Look at the seaside holiday offer.
Choose from each section to select
your holiday.
Describe your holiday choices.

6 How many different holiday selections
are possible altogether?

1 Do Workbook page 10.

2 Outside Beacon Court flats there are three parking spaces for visitors' cars. A red (**R**), a blue (**B**) and a green (**G**) car arrive at the flats.

When the blue car is parked in the first space like this

the other two cars can be parked either like this   or this

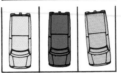

The arrangement of the cars is either B R G or B G R

Using the letters **R**, **B** and **G**, list the possible arrangements of the cars when: **(a)** the red car **(b)** the green car is parked in the first space.

3 What is the **total** number of ways in which the cars can be parked?

4 Brian places three jars on his new kitchen shelf in the order **S**, **T**, **C**.
 (a) List all the other possible ways he could order the jars on the shelf.
 (b) What is the **total** number of ways of ordering the jars on the shelf?

5 (a) Using the digits 4, 5 and 6 **each time**, how many different **three-digit** numbers do you think can be made?
 (b) List each of these numbers.

6 Louise is a lighting engineer. The picture shows six ways she can arrange four disco lights, coloured red (**R**), blue (**B**), green (**G**) and yellow (**Y**). The arrangements shown are

R	B G Y			R	G B Y		
R	B Y G			R	Y G B		
R	G Y B			R	Y B G		

List the other possible ways Louise can arrange the lights starting with

(a) the blue   **(b)** the green

(c) the yellow light.

7 How many arrangements are there **altogether**?

Ask your teacher what to do next.

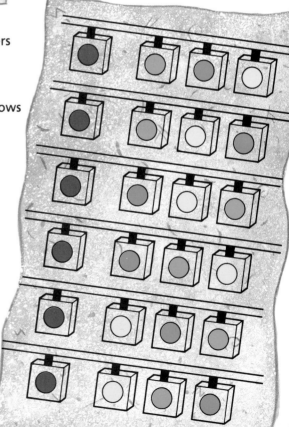

Some clothes are measured in inches and some in centimetres. You can use the table to convert from one to the other.

Waist in inches	22	23	24	25	26	27	28	29	30
Waist in cm	56	58	61	63	66	69	71	74	76

1 What are the waist measurements in centimetres for

   (a) 22 inches   (b) 25 inches   (c) 28 inches   (d) 30 inches   (e) $22\frac{1}{2}$ inches?

2 The waist sizes in inches of these trousers are marked on the hangers. What size in inches does each of these children take?

Name	Waist
Mark	74 cm
Assad	66 cm
Roberta	58 cm
Karen	61 cm
You	?

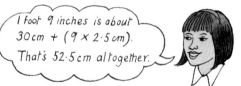

3 This red line is **one inch** long. |———— 1 inch

   Use your centimetre ruler to measure its length in centimetres to the nearest $\frac{1}{2}$ cm.

1 inch is about $2\frac{1}{2}$ cm or 2·5 cm.
1 foot is 12 inches.
1 foot is about 12 × 2·5 cm or 30 cm.

1 foot 9 inches is about 30 cm + (9 × 2·5 cm). That's 52·5 cm altogether.

Jake
4 feet

Shareen
5 feet

Laura
4 feet
6 inches

Ann
5 feet
8 inches

Wes
5 feet
11 inches

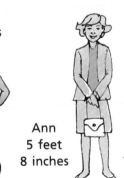

4 (a) Find the heights of Jake and Shareen in centimetres.
   (b) Use these results to help find the heights in centimetres of Laura, Ann and Wes.

5 Measure your own height in feet and inches. About how many centimetres is this?

32 Casual clothing costs

Use the prices on page 70 of the Goodies catalogue.

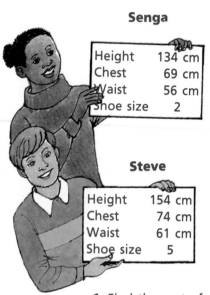

Senga

Height	134 cm
Chest	69 cm
Waist	56 cm
Shoe size	2

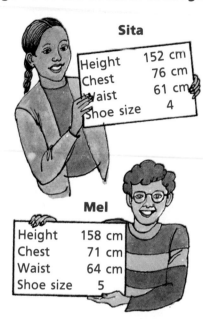

Sita

Height	152 cm
Chest	76 cm
Waist	61 cm
Shoe size	4

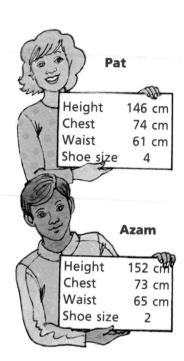

Pat

Height	146 cm
Chest	74 cm
Waist	61 cm
Shoe size	4

Steve

Height	154 cm
Chest	74 cm
Waist	61 cm
Shoe size	5

Mel

Height	158 cm
Chest	71 cm
Waist	64 cm
Shoe size	5

Azam

Height	152 cm
Chest	73 cm
Waist	65 cm
Shoe size	2

1 Find the cost of
  (a) the jacket and a pair of white jeans for Senga
  (b) a flying suit and a striped T-shirt for Sita
  (c) a cotton T-shirt and a pair of pink jeans for Pat
  (d) the jog trousers and a sweatshirt for Steve
  (e) the denim jacket and striped T-shirt for Mel
  (f) the jog jacket, blue jeans and a striped T-shirt for Azam.

2 Mel, Steve and Azam are the boys table tennis team. Part
  of their kit is a jog jacket and trousers.
  Complete Order Form 7 on **Workbook page 5** to order these
  items in the correct sizes.

3 Use the prices on page 71 of the Goodies catalogue.
  Senga, Sita and Pat are the girls badminton team.
  Use Order Form 8 on **Workbook page 5** to order sports
  shirts, shorts and shoes for the team.

4 Complete Workbook page 5 and do Workbook page 6.

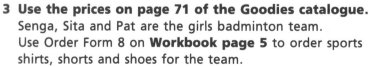

The cost of sending a parcel by post depends on its weight. **The cost of sending a parcel weighing $2\frac{1}{2}$ kg is £3·15.**

The Goodies warehouse sends out orders by parcel post.

1 Find the cost of sending each of these parcels by post.

Weight not over	Rate
1 kg	£2·00
2 kg	£2·52
3 kg	£3·15
4 kg	£3·40
5 kg	£3·60
6 kg	£4·00
7 kg	£4·15
8 kg	£4·30
9 kg	£4·80

(a)   **(b)**   **(c)**

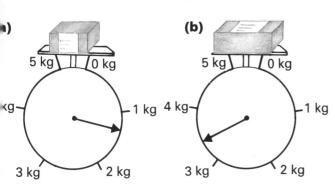
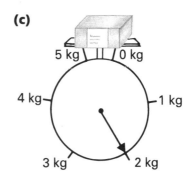

2 (a) Copy and complete this table for sending table tennis sets.
(b) How much is saved by sending both sets in one parcel instead of two separate parcels?

Number of sets in one parcel	Total weight	Postage
1	1·2 kg	
2		

3 (a) Find the cost of sending each of these catalogue items by parcel post.
(b) If all three items were sent as **one parcel**, what would be the postage charge?
(c) How much less is this than the cost for sending **three** separate parcels?

Catalogue item	Weight
Football	500 g
Table tennis set	1·2 kg
Ice skates	2·0 kg

Goodies   FREE POSTAGE OFFER – No postage charge for goods when the cash payment is over £60.

4 If the three items in question **3** were ordered from **page 69** of the **Goodies catalogue**,

(a) what would the total cash payment be?   Careful!
(b) would the free postage offer apply?

magazine Offer

save £5
on this barbecue

Usual price
£19·95

5 Michael paid £18·05 including postage for this barbecue.

(a) What did he pay for postage?
(b) What can you say about the weight of the barbecue?

Ask your teacher what to do next.

Challenge

Before paying at the checkout, Mandy Black **estimated** her shopping would cost about £5.

It should be about £5·00

1 Find the **actual** cost of her shopping. Use a calculator if you wish.

2 Was her estimate high or low? By how much?

3 Why is it a good idea to estimate the cost before paying at the checkout?

32p SHAMPOO 59p TISSUES BISCUITS 28p 48p CHEESE 18p £1·07 MELON 89p CHOCOLATE 65p

Alan Newman estimates the total cost of his shopping by taking each price **to the nearest pound**.

£1·78 is **about** £2.
£3·36 is **about** £3.

4 Use his method to **estimate** the cost of this shopping.

£2·43 FRUIT CAKE £1·78 £3·36 FANCY MILK CHOCOLATE SPAGHETTI 88p WINE £4·08 £2·88 STRAWBERRY

5 (a) Find the **actual** cost. **(b)** By how much was the estimate high or low?

Paul Johnson estimates his total cost by rounding prices **to the nearest 50p**.

£2·05 SULTANAS 48p £2·89 35p £1·39 62p 92p

6 Use his method to **estimate** the total cost of his shopping.

7 (a) Find the **actual** cost.
(b) By how much was the estimate high or low?

*62p is about 50p
£1·39 is about £1·50
92p is about £1·00*

Ruth Hebden estimates her total cost by choosing items that add together to **make pounds**.

18p and 85p is **about** £1.
£1·20 and 86p is **about** £2.

8 Use her method to **estimate** the total cost of these goods.

9 (a) Find the **actual** cost.
(b) By how much was the estimate high or low?

99p £1·20 24p 85p 86p 75p BISCUITS 18p

10 Estimate the total cost of the purchases in each basket.

(a)

£2·03 32p £1·20 £1·17
89p 67p 77p

(b)

£2·88 81p £1·86 70p 78p
£3·40 £1·71 SOAP

11 Find the **actual** cost of the purchases in each basket.

12 Assad Khan estimated that £10 would be enough to buy these goods.
   (a) What was the **actual** cost of the goods?
   (b) Which item could Assad put back to keep the total **just under** £10?

£2·21 72p £1·65 CHICKEN £3·99
32p RAVIOLI TISSUES BISCUITS 52p 95p FRUIT

Alison has £10 to spend

13 (a) Estimate the cost of the goods in Alison's trolley.
   (b) Do you think she has enough spending money? Write yes or no.
   (c) Find the **actual** total cost.
   (d) If the cost is too high, what could she put back? If the cost is low, how much money will she have left?

14 Repeat question **13** for Graham's trolley and Kay's trolley.

£1·79 £3·41 21p
£1·41 £1·32 WASHING
£2·71 80p
21p

£1·07 £3·84
£3·00 £1·19
£5·15
£4·40 £2·61

Graham has £20 in his wallet

£3·07
£5·61 £2·15
£2·21 £1·72

Kay has £15

Ask your teacher what to do next.

Each packet of breakfast cereal has a free gift of four animal picture cards which come in different sizes.

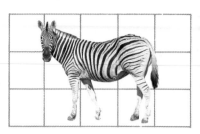

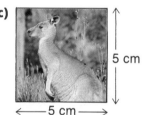

1 For each animal card find
- the number of squares in each row
- the number of rows
- the area in square centimetres.

2 Do Workbook page 42, question 1.

3 Find the area of each animal card:

(a)

4 cm

←——— 8 cm ———→

(b)

3 cm

←——— 7 cm ———→

(c)

5 cm

←—— 5 cm ——→

(d) Gorilla card $l = 9$ cm, $b = 6$ cm

(e) Polar bear card $l = 10$ cm, $b = 7.5$ cm

4 (a) Measure in centimetres the length and breadth of the lion, snake and lizard cards. Find the area of each.
(b) Which cards have the same area?

5 Draw a rectangle which has an area
(a) *less* than the snake card but greater than the lion card
(b) *equal* to the sum of the lion, snake and lizard cards.

6 Do Workbook page 11.

Jenny is a jewellery designer. She has designed a new range of earrings in coloured perspex.

This red earring is a right-angled triangle.
Its surrounding rectangle is shown.

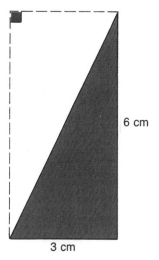

6 cm

3 cm

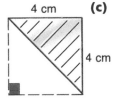

The area of the rectangle
$= 6 \times 3 = 18 \text{ cm}^2$

The area of the earring
$= \frac{1}{2}$ of $18 = 9 \text{ cm}^2$

1 The diagrams show some of Jenny's earrings and their surrounding rectangles.
Write the area of each earring.

(a)

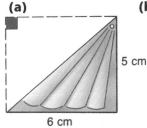

5 cm

6 cm

(b)

4 cm

4 cm

(c)

7 cm

2 cm

(d)

8 cm

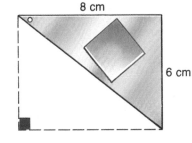

6 cm

2 (a) Measure and find the area of each of these right-angled triangle earrings.

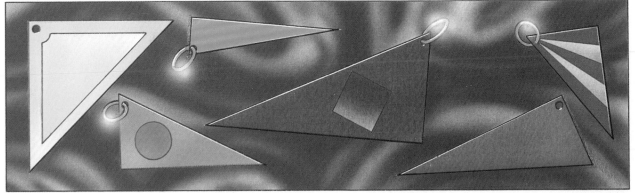

(b) Which earring has the greatest area?
(c) Which earring has the smallest area?
(d) Which earring has an area greater than the green earring and less than the blue earring?

3 On centimetre squared paper, draw three different right-angled triangle earrings each with an area of 18 cm².

4 Do Workbook page 12.

Work as a group.
You need a metre stick or tape, large sheets of paper, and sticky tape.

1 Make a paper square which has an area of about 1 square metre.

2 Work in the hall.
Use chalk to mark out a rectangle

   (a) with an area of 8 m²
   (b) with an area of 5 m² and
       breadth 50 cm.

3 Measure the length and breadth of
your classroom to the nearest metre.

   (a) About what area is your classroom
       in square metres?
   (b) About how many times will your
       classroom fit into 1 hectare?

1 hectare is 10 000 m².

4 Do Workbook page 13.

This is an aerial photograph.
It shows the centre of Edinburgh.
The area shown is 1 square kilometre (1 km²).

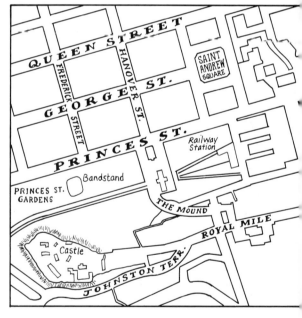

This is the street plan of the same area in
Edinburgh.

5 Find the castle and station on the street plan.
Now find them on the photograph.

6 Saint Andrew Square has an area of about 1 hectare (10 000 m²).
Estimate the area of the bandstand.

7 Do Workbook page 14.

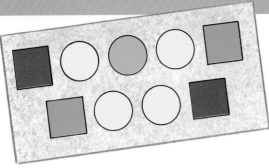

4 out of 9 disco lights are square
$\frac{4}{9}$ **are square**

1 What fraction of the disco lights are
  (a) circular   **(b)** blue   **(c)** red
  (d) yellow   **(e)** green?

2 A group of 8 boys and 7 girls go to the disco.
  (a) How many are in the group?
  (b) What fraction are • boys • girls?

3 Lisa spent £7 on her outing to the disco. She spent £3 on her ticket, £1 on travel and the rest on snacks. What fraction did she spend on
  (a) her ticket   **(b)** travel   **(c)** snacks?

2 of the 3 packs contain cola
  $\frac{2}{3}$ are cola

Each pack contains four cans.
8 of the 12 cans are cola
  $\frac{8}{12}$ are cola

$\frac{2}{3}$ is **equivalent** to $\frac{8}{12}$ $\frac{2}{3} = \frac{8}{12}$
  (×4)

4 Write **two** fractions equivalent to   **(a)** $\frac{1}{2}$ **(b)** $\frac{1}{4}$ **(c)** $\frac{2}{5}$ **(d)** $\frac{3}{8}$

5 Copy and complete: **(a)** $\frac{1}{3} = \frac{\square}{12}$ **(b)** $\frac{1}{4} = \frac{3}{\square}$ **(c)** $\frac{3}{\square} = \frac{15}{20}$ **(d)** $\frac{\square}{3} = \frac{10}{15}$

Which is greater, $\frac{2}{3}$ or $\frac{3}{4}$?

$\frac{2}{3} = \frac{8}{12}$ $\frac{9}{12}$ is greater than $\frac{8}{12}$

$\frac{3}{4} = \frac{9}{12}$ $\frac{3}{4}$ is greater than $\frac{2}{3}$

6 For each pair find which is **greater**:
  (a) $\frac{2}{3}, \frac{5}{6}$ **(b)** $\frac{2}{5}, \frac{1}{2}$ **(c)** $\frac{3}{5}, \frac{3}{4}$

7 For the disco prize draw (prize: a personal stereo) Tom sold $\frac{1}{3}$ of the tickets and Kim sold $\frac{2}{5}$ of the tickets. Who sold more tickets?

8 Simplify:
  (a) $\frac{6}{10}$ **(b)** $\frac{7}{21}$ **(c)** $\frac{9}{12}$ **(d)** $\frac{12}{18}$

$\frac{8}{12}$ can be **simplified** to $\frac{2}{3}$ $\frac{8}{12} = \frac{2}{3}$
  (÷4)

9 Kevin bought these 15 tickets for the prize draw. In simplest form, what fraction of the tickets are
  (a) red   **(b)** yellow   **(c)** green?

Remember

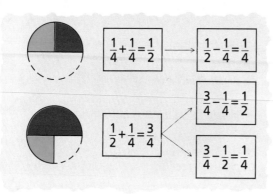

$$\frac{1}{4} + \frac{1}{4} = \frac{1}{2} \longrightarrow \frac{1}{2} - \frac{1}{4} = \frac{1}{4}$$

$$\frac{3}{4} - \frac{1}{4} = \frac{1}{2}$$

$$\frac{1}{2} + \frac{1}{4} = \frac{3}{4}$$

$$\frac{3}{4} - \frac{1}{2} = \frac{1}{4}$$

1 Copy and complete:

(a) $3\frac{1}{4} + \frac{1}{4}$ **(b)** $5\frac{1}{4} + 2\frac{1}{2}$ **(c)** $3\frac{1}{2} - \frac{1}{4}$

(d) $2\frac{3}{4} - \frac{1}{4}$ **(e)** $1\frac{3}{4} - \frac{1}{2}$ **(f)** $3\frac{1}{4} + 4\frac{1}{4}$

(g) $3\frac{1}{2} + 1\frac{1}{4}$ **(h)** $5\frac{3}{4} - 2\frac{1}{4}$ **(i)** $7\frac{1}{2} - 5\frac{1}{4}$

2 Janet is a solicitor. She walks $1\frac{1}{4}$ km from home to catch a bus to her office. The bus journey to work is $4\frac{1}{4}$ km long. How far does Janet travel from her home to her office?

3 When Janet's son, Daniel, was born he weighed $3\frac{1}{2}$ kg. On his first birthday he weighed $9\frac{3}{4}$ kg. What was his increase in weight in the year?

Remember

$$\frac{1}{2} + \frac{1}{2} = 1 \longrightarrow 1 - \frac{1}{2} = \frac{1}{2}$$

$$1 - \frac{3}{4} = \frac{1}{4}$$

$$\frac{3}{4} + \frac{1}{4} = 1$$

$$1 - \frac{1}{4} = \frac{3}{4}$$

4 Copy and complete:

(a) $3\frac{1}{2} + \frac{1}{2}$ **(b)** $\frac{1}{4} + 5\frac{3}{4}$ **(c)** $8 - \frac{1}{4}$

(d) $7 - \frac{1}{2}$ **(e)** $4 - \frac{3}{4}$ **(f)** $4\frac{1}{2} + 3\frac{1}{2}$

(g) $6 - 5\frac{1}{4}$ **(h)** $2\frac{3}{4} + 6\frac{1}{4}$ **(i)** $10 - 3\frac{3}{4}$

5 Janet goes to the supermarket. She puts her shopping in three boxes. What is the total weight of the items in

(a) the white box
(b) the yellow box
(c) the brown box
(d) all three boxes?

6 How much heavier is the total weight in the yellow box than that in the white box?

7 Janet is planning to take Daniel on holiday. Looking through her holiday brochure she finds this table showing the travelling times for four holidays.

(a) Find the total time for each journey.

(b) What is the difference in time between the longest and shortest journeys?

Holiday	Flight in hours	Coachtrip in hours
London – Costa Blanca	$2\frac{1}{4}$	$\frac{1}{2}$
Newcastle – Costa del Sol	$3\frac{1}{4}$	$\frac{1}{4}$
Birmingham – Majorca	$2\frac{1}{2}$	$1\frac{1}{2}$
Glasgow – Tenerife	$4\frac{3}{4}$	$1\frac{1}{4}$

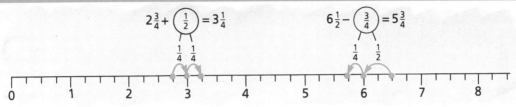

$$2\tfrac{3}{4} + \left(\tfrac{1}{2}\right) = 3\tfrac{1}{4} \qquad\qquad 6\tfrac{1}{2} - \left(\tfrac{3}{4}\right) = 5\tfrac{3}{4}$$

1 (a) $\tfrac{3}{4} + \tfrac{1}{2}$ (b) $\tfrac{3}{4} + \tfrac{3}{4}$ (c) $\tfrac{1}{2} + \tfrac{3}{4}$ (d) $1\tfrac{1}{4} - \tfrac{1}{2}$ (e) $1\tfrac{1}{2} - \tfrac{3}{4}$ (f) $1\tfrac{1}{4} - \tfrac{3}{4}$

   (g) $4\tfrac{3}{4} + \tfrac{3}{4}$ (h) $3\tfrac{1}{2} + \tfrac{3}{4}$ (i) $5\tfrac{3}{4} + \tfrac{1}{2}$ (j) $6\tfrac{1}{4} - \tfrac{3}{4}$ (k) $2\tfrac{1}{4} - \tfrac{1}{2}$ (l) $7\tfrac{1}{2} - \tfrac{3}{4}$

2 At the Highland Games, Hamish put the shot $17\tfrac{3}{4}$ m at his first attempt.

His second put was $\tfrac{3}{4}$ m further than this.

His third put was $\tfrac{3}{4}$ m further than his second put. What was the length of

(a) his second put
(b) his third put?

3 Hamish's third put broke the previous games record by $\tfrac{1}{2}$ m.

What was the previous record?

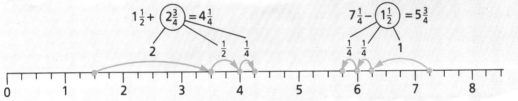

$$1\tfrac{1}{2} + \left(2\tfrac{3}{4}\right) = 4\tfrac{1}{4} \qquad\qquad 7\tfrac{1}{4} - \left(1\tfrac{1}{2}\right) = 5\tfrac{3}{4}$$

4 (a) $5\tfrac{3}{4} + 3\tfrac{3}{4}$ (b) $2\tfrac{1}{2} + 3\tfrac{3}{4}$ (c) $1\tfrac{3}{4} + 4\tfrac{1}{2}$ (d) $7\tfrac{1}{2} - 4\tfrac{3}{4}$ (e) $5\tfrac{1}{4} - 4\tfrac{1}{2}$ (f) $8\tfrac{1}{4} - 3\tfrac{3}{4}$

   (g) $7\tfrac{3}{4} + 2\tfrac{1}{2}$ (h) $6\tfrac{1}{4} - 1\tfrac{1}{2}$ (i) $4\tfrac{1}{2} + 4\tfrac{3}{4}$ (j) $3\tfrac{1}{4} - 2\tfrac{3}{4}$ (k) $1\tfrac{3}{4} + 6\tfrac{3}{4}$ (l) $2\tfrac{1}{2} - 1\tfrac{3}{4}$

5 In the 'Hurling the haggis' competition, Jamie threw to a height of $8\tfrac{1}{4}$ metres.

His sister, Fiona, threw to a height of $5\tfrac{1}{2}$ metres.

How much higher did Jamie throw than Fiona?

FRUIT DRINK
$1\tfrac{3}{4}$ l orange juice
$1\tfrac{3}{4}$ l lime juice
$4\tfrac{1}{4}$ l lemonade
water

6 Jean McTavish prepared a fruit drink for competitors in the games.

(a) She first mixed the orange juice and the lime juice.
How much juice is this altogether?

(b) She then added $4\tfrac{1}{4}$ litres of lemonade.
How much did she have in her mixture then?

(c) Finally she added water to make 10 litres of fruit drink altogether. How much water did she add?

Ask your teacher what to do next.

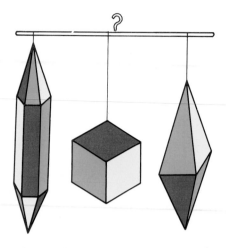

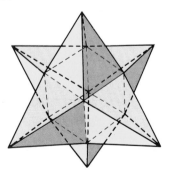

Some pupils of Gladeside School decorated their classroom with colourful shapes and mobiles.
Work in a group.
Your teacher will tell you which shapes to make.

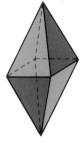

- Cut out **Workbook page 1**.
- Make the card templates you need.
- Use the templates to make card nets for your shapes.

You can make interesting mobiles and hanging shapes quite easily.

Group A

1 Make a cube and eight square pyramids.

Cube

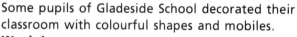

net

Square pyramid

net

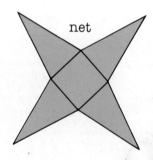

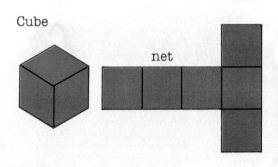

2 (a) Stick the square faces of <u>two</u> of the pyramids together to make a shape like this.
 (b) Colour the faces and hang up the shape.

3 (a) Stick the other six pyramids on the cube to make a shape like this.
 (b) Colour the faces and hang up the shape.

Octahedron

Stellated cube

Group B

1 Make a triangular prism and <u>four</u> triangular pyramids.

Triangular
prism

net

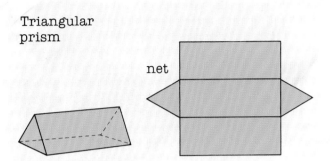

Triangular
pyramid

net

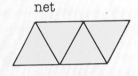

Hexahedron

2 (a) Stick two triangular pyramids together like this.
 (b) Colour the faces and hang up the shape.

3 (a) Stick the other two pyramids to the ends of the prism.
 (b) Colour the faces and hang up the shape.

Group C

1 Make a pentagonal prism and <u>four</u> pentagonal pyramids.

Pentagonal
prism

net

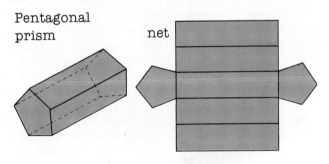

Pentagonal
pyramid

net

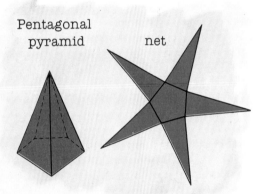

2 (a) Stick two of the pyramids base to base.
 (b) Colour the faces and hang up the shape.

3 (a) Stick the other two pyramids to the ends of the prism.
 (b) Colour the faces and hang up the shape.

Group D

1 Make a hexagonal prism and <u>four</u> hexagonal pyramids.

Hexagonal
prism

net

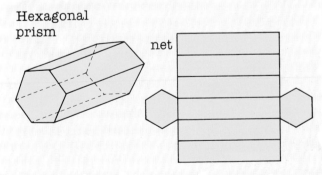

Hexagonal
pyramid

net

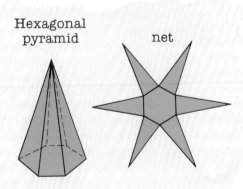

2 (a) Stick two of the pyramids base to base.
 (b) Colour the faces and hang up the shape.

3 (a) Stick the other two pyramids to the ends of the prism.
 (b) Colour the faces and hang up the shape.

You could also make mobiles out of different combinations of shapes.

Work in a group.

Here are some more complicated shapes.
Ask your teacher which of them you
should make.

You can hang your shapes
on a frame or wall bars to
display the whole
collection.

Regular octahedron

All eight faces are
equilateral triangles.

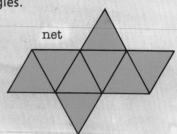

net

Dodecahedron

All twelve faces are regular
pentagons.

net

Icosahedron

All twenty faces are
equilateral triangles.

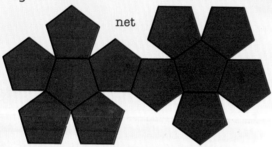

net

Truncated tetrahedron

Four faces are regular hexagons and four faces
are equilateral triangles.

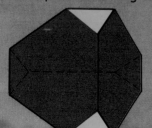

net

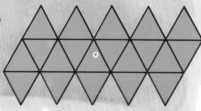

Ask your teacher what to do next.

Stellated dodecahedron

This shape can be made by
sticking *twelve* pentagonal
pyramids to the faces of a
dodecahedron.

The net for a pentagonal
pyramid is shown on *page
43*.

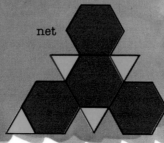

9>7 means 9 is greater than 7.   6<10 means 6 is less than 10.

1 Write the meaning of each of these:

   (a) 25>21   **(b)** 47<51   **(c)** 46=80−34   **(d)** 510>501   **(e)** 3×7>4×5

2 Write each statement using one of the symbols <, > or =

   (a) 19 is greater than 15   **(b)** 12 is less than 21   **(c)** 8 is equal to 24÷3
   (d) 405 is less than 504   **(e)** 6×7 is greater than 8×5

3 For the pair of numbers 35 and 41 **two** statements can be written using < and >.
   For example: 41>35 **and** 35<41.

   Write two statements for each of these pairs:

   (a) 6 and 16   **(b)** 87 and 78   **(c)** 405 and 450   **(d)** 1010 and 1101
   (e) 6×5 and 4×8   **(f)** 49÷7 and 54÷6   **(g)** 2×6 and 81÷9

4 Four pupils picked these winning numbers in a lucky number draw.

   Joe **13**   Kim **24**   Zoe **27**   Tom **17**

   Find each pupil's prize by passing the lucky numbers through the decision tree.

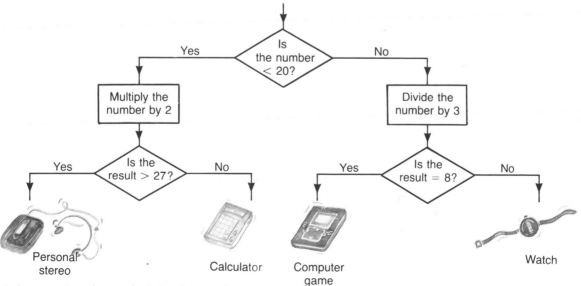

Ask your teacher what to do next.

1 Prizes are given to car drivers with a E, F or G registration letter and a lucky number.
Which of these registrations have lucky numbers?

| F 614 YEP | E 888 KJD | G 302 TYY |

| E 503 KJD | G 183 UHM | F 205 YCY |

CAR PARK
LUCKY NUMBERS

E Number divides exactly by 4

F Number has remainder 1 when divided by 3

G Number has remainder 5 when divided by 9

2 Each ticket for the Wheel of Fortune has a four-digit number. To win a prize this number must be exactly divisible by the number shown by the pointer.
Which of these are winning numbers?

6674
5738
2583
4710

Wheel of Fortune

8659
3984
5362
6309

Wheel of Fortune

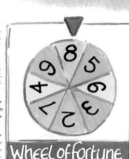

8992
5375
4646
2600

Wheel of fortune

3 2500 sandwiches were delivered to the tea tent.

(a) $\frac{1}{2}$ of the sandwiches had a ham filling

$\frac{1}{5}$ had a salad filling and

$\frac{1}{4}$ had a cheese filling.

The rest had an egg filling.
How many were there of each of the four types of sandwich?

(b) Tracy's dog ate 10 of the sandwiches.
The rest were put on plates, 3 to each plate.
How many plates of sandwiches were made up?

4 875 scones and 855 cakes were also delivered to the tent.
(a) The scones were in 7 equal batches.
How many were in each batch?
(b) The cakes were packed in boxes of 9.
How many boxes were there?

5 One class arranged 178 chairs in the tea tent, setting out 5 to each table.
(a) How many tables were there?
(b) How many chairs were left?

6 (a) 1000 stickers were needed for the souvenir stall.
They are supplied with 6 stickers on a sheet.
How many sheets had to be ordered?
(b) The school paid £405 for boxes of mugs costing £9 per box.
There are 8 mugs in a box.
How many mugs did the school buy?

1 Prizes are given to parents who are successful in the Division Challenge.
These are the tests. Find the answers.

CHALLENGE A

(a) $3\overline{)79\cdot2}$ **(b)** $7\overline{)87\cdot5}$

(c) $785\cdot7 \div 9$ **(d)** $499\cdot2 \div 6$

(e) $7\overline{)765\cdot8}$ **(f)** $9\overline{)905\cdot4}$

(g) $\frac{1}{2}$ of 95 **(h)** $\frac{1}{10}$ of 178

(i) $4\overline{)390\cdot0}$ **(j)** $5\overline{)104}$

CHALLENGE B

(a) $2\overline{)7\cdot28}$ **(b)** $4\overline{)3\cdot88}$

(c) $9\cdot72 \div 9$ **(d)** $88\cdot41 \div 3$

(e) $8\overline{)43\cdot76}$ **(f)** $6\overline{)48\cdot18}$

(g) $\frac{1}{2}$ of 72·90 **(h)** $\frac{1}{10}$ of 73·1

(i) $5\overline{)36\cdot2}$ **(j)** $4\overline{)59}$

DIVISION CHALLENGE
FOR PARENTS
ENTRY : 50p
NO CALCULATORS ALLOWED

PRIZES!

2 Dave Evans ran the record stall. He charged 10p to
hear a favourite record. He collected £5·80. How
many records did he play?

3 Jan sold 10 quiz sheets and collected £2·50.
How much was each quiz sheet?

4 Jane Reid, the school
secretary, collected
these takings from
four stallholders.
Find the average
amount taken.

£41·50 SOUVENIRS

£20·35 BOOKS

£7·30 RECORDS

£65·45 CAKES

5 In the tug-o-war, 10 pupils pulled against 5 parents.
  (a) The total weight of the pupils was 352 kg.
    Find their average weight.
  (b) The weights of the parents were 68·8 kg, 75 kg, 71·3 kg,
    65·8 kg and 67·1 kg. Find their average weight.

6 Imran spent $2\frac{3}{4}$ hours
giving children rides on
his pony.
Each ride lasted 5
minutes. How many
rides did he give?

7 (a) The tea tent is 11 metres wide.
    Six tables are placed across the tent
    to make a counter, leaving a gap of
    1·7 metres for a passageway.
    What is the width in metres and
    centimetres of each table?
  (b) The height of a stack of cake boxes
    is 1·28 metres.
    Each box is 8 centimetres high. How
    many boxes are there in the stack?

72p for 4

What is the cost of **one** apple when you buy a bag of four?

Number of apples	Cost in pence
4	72
1	72 ÷ 4 = **18**

```
    18
  4 )72
```

The cost of one apple is **18p**.

Guess the weight of one ball.

1 Find the cost of **one** apple in each of these bags.

	(a)	(b)	(c)	(d)
Cost in pence	57	84	91	99
Number in bag	3	6	7	11

2 To find the winning guesses these bags of balls were weighed. Use the information in this table to calculate the weight of **one** of each kind of ball.

	Football	Cricket	Tennis	Golf
Weight in grams	490	812	340	445
Number of balls	4	5	8	10

3 A go-kart track was set up at the fair. The distance travelled in 6 laps of the track is 915 metres. Find the distance travelled in **(a)** 1 lap **(b)** 2 laps **(c)** 3 laps **(d)** 5 laps.

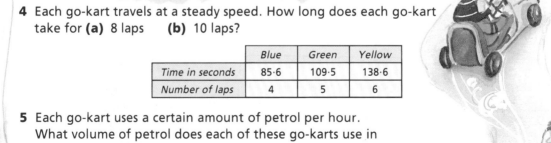

The red go-kart completes 5 laps in 114 seconds. At this speed, how long does it take for 8 laps?

Number of laps	Time in seconds
5	114
1	114 ÷ 5 = 22·8
8	22·8 × 8 = **182·4**

```
    22·8
  5 )114·0
```

```
   22·8
  ×   8
  182·4
```

Time for 8 laps is **182·4 seconds**.

4 Each go-kart travels at a steady speed. How long does each go-kart take for **(a)** 8 laps **(b)** 10 laps?

	Blue	Green	Yellow
Time in seconds	85·6	109·5	138·6
Number of laps	4	5	6

5 Each go-kart uses a certain amount of petrol per hour. What volume of petrol does each of these go-karts use in

(a) 4 hours **(b)** 6 hours?

	Blue	Green	Yellow
Petrol used in litres	9·17	10·16	10·35
Number of hours	7	8	9

Ask your teacher what to do next.

Here are four different types of angles.

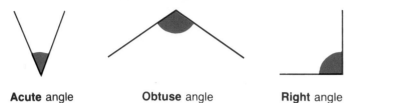

Acute angle **Obtuse** angle **Right** angle **Reflex** angle

1 What type of angle is

(a) less than 90° (b) equal to 90°

(c) between 90° and 180° (d) between 180° and 360°?

2 For each of the angles marked **a** to **q** in the pictures below
write down whether it is **acute**, **obtuse**, **right** or **reflex**.

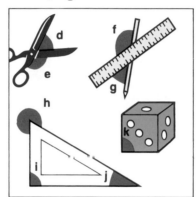

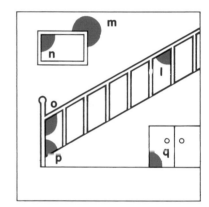

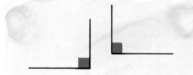

Two right angles fit
together like this to make a
straight angle.
A straight angle is 180°.

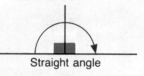

Straight angle

3 List pairs of compass directions
which make straight angles.
For example: **N and S**

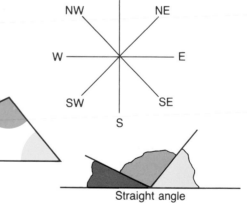

4 (a) On plain paper
- draw a large triangle
- colour the corners as shown
- cut out your triangle
- tear off each corner
- place the corners together like this.

Straight angle

(b) Copy and complete:
The sum of the angles of a triangle is a _____ angle or _____°.

5 (a) Find out which of these shapes make tilings that have straight angles:
square, rhombus, kite, triangle, hexagon, parallelogram, octagon.

(b) Display your tilings on the wall.

Challenge

A plumb line
hangs vertically.
The string is
vertical.

A spirit level shows when a surface is
horizontal like the horizon.

In this room
the floor is
horizontal
and the walls
are **vertical**.

1 Write horizontal or vertical for each of these **surfaces**:

   (a) the sides of the TV set   **(b)** the table top

   (c) the shelves of the bookcase   **(d)** the sides of the bookcase.

2 Write horizontal or vertical for each of these **lines**:

   (a) the light flex   **(b)** the top edge of the radiator

   (c) the legs of the table   **(d)** the line where the walls meet.

3 Beteen 1.50 pm and 3.05 pm when is the **minute hand**

   (a) horizontal   **(b)** vertical?

4 How many of the sword blades on the wall are

   (a) horizontal   **(b)** vertical   **(c)** neither horizontal nor vertical?

5 Write horizontal or vertical for each of these:

   (a) a lamp post   **(b)** the surface of a still pond

   (c) a flag pole   **(d)** the cross bar of goal posts

   (e) the walls of a house   **(f)** the top surface of a glass of milk

   (g) a window sill   **(h)** the cord on a bathroom light switch

6 Make and test a simple • plumb line • spirit level.

1 (a) Make a pair of parallel lines by drawing a line on each side of your ruler.

(b) Turn your ruler and draw another pair of parallel lines to make a rhombus.

2 In this sketch, which colour of lines are

(a) vertical

(b) horizontal

(c) parallel

(d) none of these?

Two lines which meet at right angles are **perpendicular**.

Horizontal and vertical lines which meet are **perpendicular**.

3 Fix two straws together so that they are perpendicular.

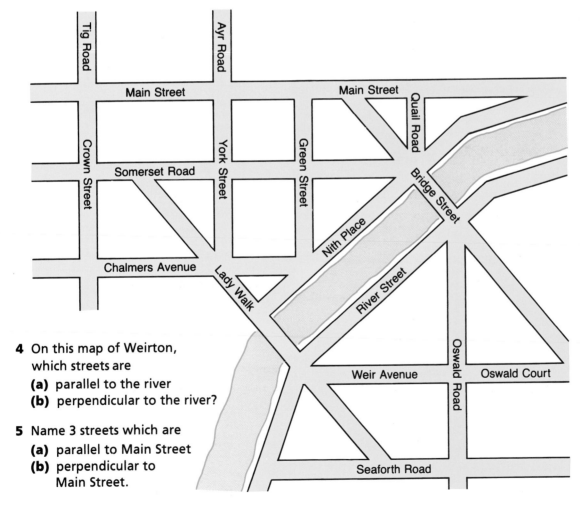

4 On this map of Weirton, which streets are

(a) parallel to the river

(b) perpendicular to the river?

5 Name 3 streets which are

(a) parallel to Main Street

(b) perpendicular to Main Street.

6 Go to Workbook page 16.

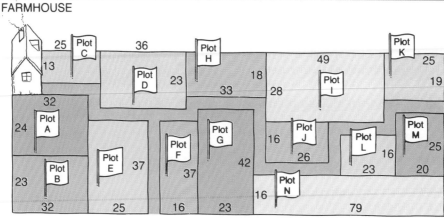

FARMHOUSE

Mary and Stephen Stacey run Grange Farm.
Above is a plan of one part of the farm. The lengths are in metres.

1 Stephen is applying for a rent review. He needs to work
out the area of each plot but has lost his calculator.

```
The area of              32
Plot A is              × 24
(32 × 24) m²            128
                       640
                       ─────
                       768  ──────→  Area is 768 m².
```

Without a calculator, find the areas of Plots B, C, D, E and F.

2 Find the area of a rectangular plot which measures

   (a) 79 m by 65 m   **(b)** 154 m by 68 m   **(c)** 236 m by 87 m   **(d)** 98 m by 378 m

3 Mary helps Stephen with his calculations. She uses a multiplication table:

The area of
Plot G is
(42 × 23) m²

X	20	3
40	800	120
2	40	6

```
      800
      120
       40
    +   6
    ─────
      966  ──────→  Area is 966 m².
```

Use Mary's method to find the areas of Plots H to N.

4 Six people work on the farm. Mary calculates each of
their wages like this.

```
The wage for          447p
J. Brown is          × 36
£4·47 × 36          ──────
                     2682
                  + 13410
                  ────────
                   16092p  ──→ Wage is £160·92.
```

Workers' wages		
Name	Hourly rate	No. of hours
J. Brown	£4·47	36
D. Stokes	£4·47	29
G. Good	£4·65	52
A. Moore	£5·86	47
C. Clay	£5·09	38
P. Peat	£2·80	43

Calculate the wage for each of the other workers.

Ask your teacher what to do next.

I ordered 416 bushes

There is space for 13 equal rows. How many will we plant in each row?

416 ÷ 13

Mark's method

```
13 | 416        ← 416 bushes
   - 130 | 10 ←
     286        ← 286 bushes left    10 bushes to
   - 130 | 10 ←                      each row uses
     156        ← 156 bushes left    13 × 10 = 130
   - 130 | 10 ←                      bushes
      26        ← 26 bushes left
   -  13 | 1 ←                       1 bush to
      13        ← 13 bushes left      each row uses
   -  13 | 1 ←                        13 × 1 = 13
          | 32                        bushes
```

Dianne's method

```
13 | 416        ← 416 bushes        30 bushes to
   - 390 | 30 ←                     each row uses
      26        ← 26 bushes left     13 × 30 = 390 bushes
   -  26 | 2 ←
          | 32                       2 bushes to
                                     each row uses
                                     13 × 2 = 26 bushes
```

Mark used five subtractions.   Dianne used two subtractions.

There are **32** bushes in each row.

1 Use Mark's or Dianne's method to find how many plants are in each row.

	Pansies	Daisies	Roses	Heathers
No. of plants	437	759	930	858
No. of rows	19	23	62	39

In questions 2, 3 and 4 find each answer and write how many subtractions you needed. Use as few as possible.

2 Mark buys 960 bags of peat and stacks them in sixty-fours. How many stacks are there?

3 How many stacks are there for each of these products?

	Peat	Grit	Fertiliser	Sand
No. of bags	984	832	486	768
No. in each stack	24	16	18	48

4 (a) Dianne orders 5400 litres of forest bark in 45-litre bags. How many bags has she ordered?
(b) Mark orders 2520 kg of moss killer in 12 kg boxes. How many boxes has he ordered?
(c) Dianne paid £4590 for 34 greenhouse heaters. How much did she pay for each heater?

Ask your teacher what to do next.

1 The path to the front door of each house has a row of grey slabs between two rows of white slabs.

This path has 3 grey slabs and 6 white slabs.

(a) Copy and complete this table for paths with
- 4 grey slabs
- 5 grey slabs
- 10 grey slabs
- 20 grey slabs.

Number of grey slabs	Number of white slabs
3 ⟶	6

(b) Describe how to find the number of white slabs when you know the number of grey slabs.

2 Each pavement is made from slabs and kerbstones. Kerbstones are placed along one side and at each end of the pavement. This pavement has 5 slabs and 7 kerbstones.

(a) Copy and complete this table for
- 3 slabs
- 4 slabs
- 10 slabs
- 20 slabs.

Number of slabs	Number of kerbstones
5 ⟶	7

(b) Explain how to find the number of kerbstones when you know the number of slabs.

3 Two houses side by side have 1 joining wall.

Three houses side by side have 2 joining walls.

joining wall

(a) Copy and complete this table for
- 4 houses
- 5 houses
- 10 houses
- 30 houses.

Number of houses	Number of joining walls
2 ⟶	1
3 ⟶	2

(b) Describe how to find the number of joining walls when you know the number of houses.

4 Do Workbook page 17.

We may be doing a lot more sunbathing if global warming has an effect! What do you think?

The graph shows the outside temperature, in degrees Celsius, at noon each day for two weeks in London.

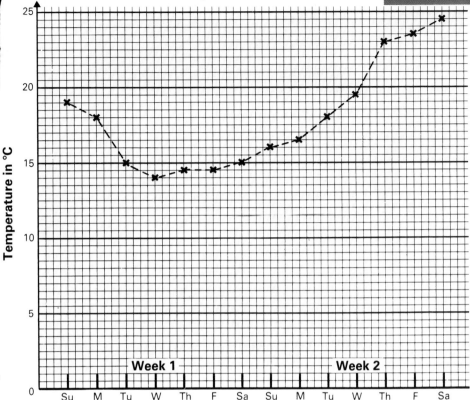

Temperatures at noon

1 (a) Which day had the *highest* and which day had the *lowest* noon temperatures?
   (b) What were these temperatures?

2 Which season of the year do you think it was?

3 The dotted lines show the **trend** in the noon temperatures. The temperatures fall at the beginning, level off, and then rise towards the end of the two weeks.
   (a) Between which two **consecutive** days did the greatest
      • fall   • rise in noon temperatures occur?
   (b) By how much did the temperatures change?

4 Here is the **trend** graph for a different fortnight in London.
   (a) Write about the trends it shows.
   (b) Which season of the year do you think it was?

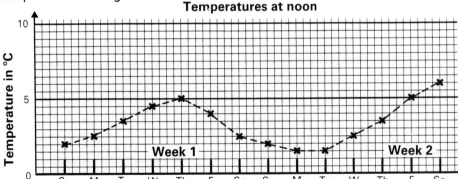

Temperatures at noon

5 (a) Draw the trend graph for these daily noon temperatures for two weeks.
   (b) Write about the trends your graph shows.

	Day of the week	Su	M	Tu	W	Th	F	Sa
Week 1	Noon temp. in °C	9	10·5	10	11·5	12	14	16
Week 2	Noon temp. in °C	17·5	16	15	14·5	12·5	12	10

6 Record daily the outside noon temperature for two weeks. Draw a trend graph of your results.

Challenge

1 The Cliffords hire a small launch, *Kitty*.
They cruise at a steady speed of 16 km per hour.
How far do they cruise in two hours?

2 This table shows the distance travelled by *Kitty*
at different times during the cruise.

Time in hours	0	1	2
Distance in km	0	16	32

Cruising on Kitty

The information in the table has been used to draw
this **straight-line** graph. What does each small interval represent on
(a) the time axis **(b)** the distance axis?

3 (a) The times taken by *Kitty* to
cruise between some islands are
shown below.
Use the graph. Find the distance
between each pair of islands.

(b) The distances between some other
islands are shown below.
Use the graph. Find the time taken
by *Kitty* to cruise between
each pair of islands.

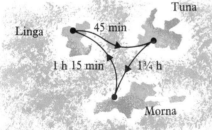

4 Jane and her friends hire the launch *Hawk*.
They cruise at a steady speed of **20 km
per hour**.

Time in hours	0	1	5
Distance in km	0		

(a) Copy and complete this table of cruise
times and distances.
(b) Use the information in your table to draw a straight-line
graph on ½ cm squared paper. Label each axis as shown.
Choose your own scale for the distance axis.

Use your graph.
5 Find the distance travelled by *Hawk* in **(a)** 3 hours **(b)** $4\frac{1}{2}$ hours.

6 Find the time taken by *Hawk* to travel **(a)** 30 km **(b)** 70 km.

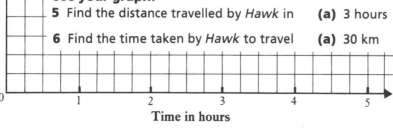

7 Do Workbook page 18, questions 1, 2 and 3.

Alan listens to the weather forecast on the *Lucy*'s radio . . .

. . . the temperature will reach 20 degrees Celsius (20°C) or 68 degrees Fahrenheit (68°F)

1 The table shows three temperatures each recorded in two scales.

Temperature in °F	32	68	104
Temperature in °C	0	20	40

This information has been used to draw a **conversion** graph.

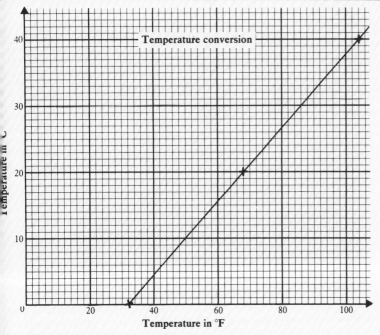

2 What does one small interval represent on
 (a) the Celsius axis
 (b) the Fahrenheit axis?

Use the graph.

3 Convert these temperatures to °F:
 (a) 30°C **(b)** 15°C.

4 Convert these temperatures to °C:
 (a) 50°F **(b)** 95°F.

5 The *Lucy* is in the Irish Sea. What season is it most likely to be when the temperature at 2.00 pm is
 (a) 25°C **(b)** 36°F?

6 Do Workbook page 18, questions 5 and 6.

7 The graph shows the volume of petrol in *Lucy*'s tank from the start to the finish of Alan's cruise.
 What does one small interval represent on
 (a) the volume axis **(b)** the time axis?

8 (a) What were the starting and finishing times of the cruise?
 (b) How long did the cruise last?

9 What volume of petrol was in *Lucy*'s tank
 (a) at the start **(b)** after 1 hour
 (c) after 2 hours **(d)** at the finish of the cruise?

10 (a) What volume of petrol was used during the cruise?
 (b) *Lucy* travelled 4 km for each litre of petrol used. What was the length of the cruise in kilometres?
 (c) What was *Lucy*'s average speed in km per hour?

Ask your teacher what to do next.

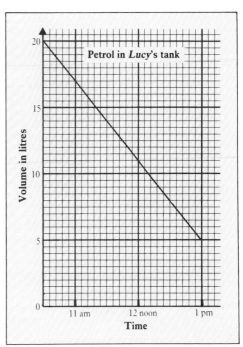

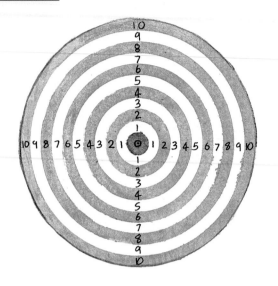

A game for two players.

This is how you play, starting with 10 .

- Write the starting number. ⟶ 10
- The first player subtracts 1 **or** 2. ⟶ −1
                                                    9
- The second player subtracts 1 **or** 2. ⟶ −2

- In turn, each player subtracts 1 **or** 2.   7

The winner is the player who subtracts to reach zero.

Work with a partner.

1 (a) Play Target Zero several times, starting with 10.
(b) Write about the winning strategy.

2 (a) Try the strategy for these starting numbers:

14   20   25

(b) Is it always possible for the first player to win? Explain.
(c) Try to find a starting number where the first player **cannot** be sure of winning.

3 In a second version of Target Zero each player can subtract 1 **or** 2 **or** 3.
(a) Play this version of the game several times.
(b) Write about the winning strategy.

4 (a) Make up a third version of Target Zero and play it with your partner.
(b) Write about the winning strategy.

Ask your teacher what to do next.

Pat Duncan sells hand-made chocolates.
There are 16 nut supremes in each box. How many
boxes can Pat fill from a batch of 4048 nut supremes?

Enter `4048`. Press `÷` `1` `6` `=` to give `253`

She can fill **253 boxes**.

1 How many boxes can Pat fill from these four batches of nut supremes:
   (a) 4848   **(b)** 5552   **(c)** 9296   **(d)** 8672?

2 How many boxes of mints can she fill from these batches:
   (a) 5280   **(b)** 8352   **(c)** 10 752   **(d)** 13 152?

3 How many boxes of truffles can she fill from these batches:
   (a) 6048   **(b)** 6930   **(c)** 7650   **(d)** 8244?

4 How many packets can she fill from these batches of
   chocolate gingers:
   (a) 3375   **(b)** 4320   **(c)** 5055   **(d)** 5640?

5 Pat delivers her chocolates to local shops in large cartons.
   Find the average weight in grams of
   (a) one box of nut supremes   **(b)** one box of mints
   (c) one box of truffles   **(d)** one packet of chocolate gingers.

6 Find the average weight in grams of
   (a) one nut supreme
   (b) one mint
   (c) one truffle
   (d) one chocolate ginger.

7 Pat sends out accounts each month. Find the cost of
   (a) one box of nut supremes   **(b)** one box of mints
   (c) one box of truffles   **(d)** one box of
                                      chocolate gingers.

Pat Duncan —
Chocolates Account
55 boxes of nut supremes £96·80
30 boxes of mints £50·40
25 boxes of truffles £63
32 boxes of chocolate
gingers £76·80

8 Find the cost of
   (a) one nut supreme   **(b)** one mint
   (c) one truffle   **(d)** one chocolate
                                ginger.

PART
THREE

At Lomond School there are 941 pupils and 69 teachers.

To find the **average** or **mean** number of pupils per teacher:

Enter 941. Press ÷ 6 9 = to give 13.637681   13·637681

You can show 13·637 681 on a numberline.
It is between 13 and 14.
It is nearer **14**.

13   13·6   14

The average or mean number of pupils per teacher = **14 to the nearest whole number.**

1 Do Workbook page 19, question 1.

2 At Lomond School all the pupils
in the first four years take
maths. For each year, find the
average number of pupils
per maths class, correct to the
nearest whole number.

	Total number of pupils	Number of maths classes
First year	183	7
Second year	195	7
Third year	267	9
Fourth year	219	8

The pupils of Class 3B
measured their weights,
heights and handspans.
The **totals** of these
measurements are given
in the table.

	Number of pupils	Total weights	Total heights	Total handspans
Girls	14	683 kg	2213 cm	260 cm
Boys	17	861 kg	2729 cm	341 cm

3 For the **girls** of Class 3B, find to the nearest whole number
the mean   **(a)** weight   **(b)** height   **(c)** handspan.

4 For the **boys** of Class 3B, find to the nearest whole number
the mean   **(a)** weight   **(b)** height   **(c)** handspan.

5 For all of **Class 3B**, find to the nearest whole number
the mean   **(a)** weight   **(b)** height   **(c)** handspan.

6 Find out the mean handspan of **your**
class to the nearest whole centimetre.

The keys on a keyboard are 2 cm wide.
On average, how many of these keys
can a pupil in your class span?

What do you think is the top-selling item at your school tuck shop?

Jean Martin runs the tuck shop. In October Jean sold 199 packets of plain crisps.

A full box of plain crisps contains 48 packets.

To find the number of full boxes used:

Enter **199.** Press **÷ 4 8 =** to give **4.1458333**

4 full boxes

4 full boxes hold 192 packets

To find the number of packets sold from the next box:

Enter **4.** Press **x 4 8 =** to give **192.**

7 packets were sold from the next box

199 − 192 = 7

1 **Do Workbook page 19, question 3.**

2 Tuck shop items which sold well in November are shown in the table. For each item find
 (a) the number of full boxes used
 (b) the number sold from the next box
 (c) the number of boxes which had to be opened.

Item	Number of packets sold	Number in one full box
Peanuts	140	24
Crisp bars	137	15
Buttermix	128	12

3 Lomond School has 4 houses.
 (a) How many pupils would you expect to be in each house?
 (b) How many **first year** pupils would you expect to be in each house?

4 Each first year class has either 31 or 32 pupils.
 (a) How many first year classes are there?
 (b) How many of these have 32 pupils?

Ros Evans is head of Mathematics. She wants to buy 190 textbooks and 380 exercise books for next term.

5 Textbooks are sold in packets of twelve but can also be bought singly.
 (a) How many full packets must Ros Evans order?
 (b) How many single textbooks must she order?

6 Exercise books are sold in packets of twenty-five and **cannot** be bought singly.
 (a) How many full packets must she buy?
 (b) How many spare exercise books will there be?

Ask your teacher what to do next.

A logo is a symbol. This is the British Rail lo[go]

1 Any design, when rotated, can fill its own outline **once** or **more than once** in one full turn.

- Trace the British Rail logo.
- Rotate your tracing on top of the logo to find how often it fits in one full turn.
  Count the starting position once only.
- Copy and complete:

  It fits _____ times in one full turn.

2 Repeat question **1** for these designs.

(a)   **(b)**   **(c)**   **(d)**

3 Find, by tracing, how many times in one full turn each car badge fits its own outline.

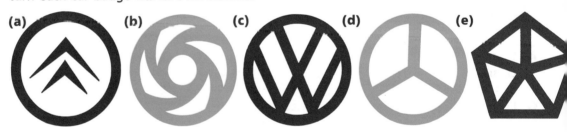

(a) **(b)** **(c)** **(d)** **(e)**

4 Find, by tracing, how many times in one full turn each road sign fits its own outline.

(a)  **(b)**   **(c)**

(d)  **(e)**   **(f)**

5 (a) Find out what each of these road signs means.
(b) Make a display of road signs with their meanings.

Sailors use these international **code flags** to give information to other ships. The flags represent the letters of the alphabet. Most of them also have special meanings. Some of these are given below.

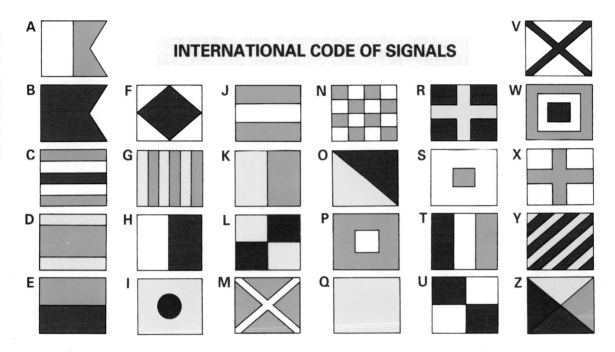

INTERNATIONAL CODE OF SIGNALS

A	Diver down – keep well clear.	J	On fire – dangerous cargo, keep well clear.

A Diver down – keep well clear.
C Yes (affirmative).
G I require a pilot.

J On fire – dangerous cargo, keep well clear.
M My vessel is stopped.
N No (negative).
O Man overboard.

U You are running into danger.
W I require medical assistance.
Z I require a tug.

1 What information is given when each of these flags is flying? **(a)** **(b)** **(c)**

2 Draw the flag which should be flown to show
   (a) man overboard
   (b) on fire – dangerous cargo, keep well clear
   (c) I require medical assistance.

3 This flag is flying correctly. Here the flag is upside down.

List all the flags which look different when flown upside down.

4 List six flags which, **when rotated**, fit their outline **twice** in one full turn.

5 Go to Workbook page 28.

Pizza pieces

Dave and two friends buy a take-away pizza
to eat while watching a video.

They each eat $\frac{1}{4}$ of the pizza.

Altogether they eat $3 \times \frac{1}{4}$ ⟶ 3 quarters
$= \frac{3}{4}$ of the pizza.

1 Write a multiplication and find each total amount.

(a) *Volume in litres.*
4 bottles each
containing $\frac{1}{5}$ litre.

(b) *Quantity of cake.*
5 slices of cake,
each $\frac{1}{6}$ of whole cake.

(c) *Time in seconds.*
2 flashes of lightning
each lasting $\frac{2}{5}$ second.

(d) *Weight in kilograms.*
2 parcels each
weighing $\frac{3}{10}$ kg.

There are 8 quarter tarts
on the tray.

$8 \times \frac{1}{4} = \frac{8}{4} = 2$

2 Find

(a) $6 \times \frac{1}{2}$ **(b)** $12 \times \frac{1}{4}$ **(c)** $10 \times \frac{1}{5}$

(d) $9 \times \frac{1}{3}$ **(e)** $8 \times \frac{1}{2}$ **(f)** $12 \times \frac{1}{6}$

Each can of oil holds $\frac{8}{10}$ litres .

Total volume $= 3 \times \frac{8}{10}$

$= \frac{24}{10}$

$= 2\frac{4}{10}$

$= 2\frac{2}{5}$ litres

*3 × 8 tenths
is 24 tenths*

3 Multiply to find each total amount.

(a) *Weight in kilograms.*

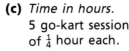

LAWN SEED $\frac{3}{4}$ kg

(b) *Volume in litres.*

PAINT $\frac{1}{2}$ litre

(c) *Time in hours.*
5 go-kart sessions
of $\frac{1}{4}$ hour each.

GO-KART

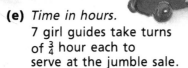

(d) *Distance in kilometres.*
Relay – 4 swimmers
swim $\frac{2}{5}$ km each.

(e) *Time in hours.*
7 girl guides take turns
of $\frac{3}{4}$ hour each to
serve at the jumble sale.

(f) *Distance in kilometres.*
Sports Car Race
8 laps of $\frac{7}{10}$ km.

She calculates the total distance she jogs
in a week, **mentally**.

$3 \times 5\frac{1}{4}$ km

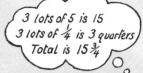

*3 lots of 5 is 15
3 lots of $\frac{1}{4}$ is 3 quarters
Total is $15\frac{3}{4}$*

$= \mathbf{15\frac{3}{4}}$ **km**

Fiona jogs a distance of $5\frac{1}{4}$ kilometres,
three times a week.

1 Find mentally the total distance each person jogs:

   (a) Dave jogs $6\frac{1}{5}$ km three times a week.   **(b)** Syeda jogs $3\frac{1}{10}$ km seven times a week.

   (c) Mark jogs $5\frac{1}{2}$ km twice a week.   **(d)** Eileen jogs $7\frac{1}{4}$ km four times a week.

2 Multiply mentally to find each total amount:

   (a) *Distance in kilometres.*   **(b)** *Weight in kilograms.*
   4 circuits of a $1\frac{1}{5}$ km   3 cans of beans each weighing
   cross country run. $1\frac{3}{10}$ kg.

   (c) *Time in hours.*   **(d)** *Volume in litres.*
   4 athletics training
   sessions of $2\frac{1}{4}$ hours.

3 Do these mentally:

   (a) $2 \times 3\frac{1}{3}$ **(b)** $3 \times 1\frac{1}{4}$ **(c)** $7 \times 1\frac{1}{10}$ **(d)** $4 \times 6\frac{1}{5}$ **(e)** $3 \times 2\frac{3}{10}$ **(f)** $8 \times 5\frac{1}{4}$

Don swims for $2\frac{3}{4}$ hours seven times
a week.

He calculates his total time like this:

$$\begin{aligned}
\textbf{Total time} &= 7 \times 2\frac{3}{4} \\
&= (7 \times 2) + (7 \times \frac{3}{4}) \\
&= 14 + \frac{21}{4} \\
&= 14 + 5\frac{1}{4} \\
&= \mathbf{19\frac{1}{4}} \textbf{ hours}
\end{aligned}$$

4 Use this method to find the total time for

   (a) 5 swims of $1\frac{1}{4}$ hours   **(b)** 6 swims of $2\frac{1}{2}$ hours   **(c)** 3 swims of $1\frac{3}{4}$ hours.

5 Multiply to find each total amount:

   (a) *Distance in kilometres.*   **(b)** *Weight in tonnes.*
   Kirsty walks $1\frac{3}{5}$ km   5 trucks each weighing $1\frac{1}{4}$ tonnes.
   7 times a week.

   (c) *Volume in litres.*   **(d)** *Weight in kilograms.*
   9 buckets each containing
   $4\frac{3}{10}$ litres of water.

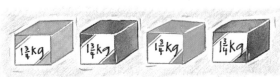

Find $\frac{1}{6}$ of 30.   To find $\frac{1}{6}$ divide by 6.

$\frac{1}{6}$ of 30 = 5

1 Find mentally
  (a) $\frac{1}{10}$ of 90   (b) $\frac{1}{5}$ of 35   (c) $\frac{1}{4}$ of 28
  (d) $\frac{1}{3}$ of 18   (e) $\frac{1}{8}$ of 56   (f) $\frac{1}{6}$ of 42

2 Silver's fitness club has 40 adults and
16 juniors. The club advertised for new
members.
  (a) The number of adults increased by $\frac{1}{5}$.
    How many more adults was this?
  (b) The number of juniors increased by $\frac{1}{4}$.
    How many more juniors was this?
  (c) What was the new **total** membership?

3 The club bought new apparatus costing
£245.
Only $\frac{1}{7}$ of this amount was paid for from
club funds. The rest was borrowed.
How much was
  (a) paid from club funds
  (b) borrowed?

Find $\frac{1}{5}$ of 4 metres.

$\frac{1}{5}$ of 4 metres
$= \frac{1}{5}$ of 400 cm
$= 80$ centimetres

$5\overline{)400}$ → 80

4 Find
  (a) $\frac{1}{4}$ of 3 metres (in centimetres)
  (b) $\frac{1}{3}$ of 2 hours (in minutes)
  (c) $\frac{1}{5}$ of 4 litres (in millilitres)
  (d) $\frac{1}{8}$ of 5 kilograms (in grams).

5 An evening session at Silver's lasts for 3 hours.
One fifth of this time is used for floor exercises.
How much time is used for floor exercises?

Use a calculator for questions 6 and 7.

Find $\frac{1}{4}$ of 2316.   Enter **2316.**
Press **÷ 4 =**
to give **579.**

6 Find
  (a) $\frac{1}{3}$ of 1665   (b) $\frac{1}{2}$ of 38 158
  (c) $\frac{1}{5}$ of £87 000   (d) $\frac{1}{6}$ of £102 000
  (e) $\frac{1}{4}$ of 7850 litres   (f) $\frac{1}{8}$ of 42 200 m²

7 Three members of Silver's club drove
1608 km to a body-building
competition in France.
Angela drove for $\frac{1}{4}$ of the journey and
Tom drove for $\frac{1}{3}$ of the journey.
Ajay drove for the remainder of the
journey.
How far did each person drive?

Find $\frac{3}{5}$ of 40.

To find 1 fifth divide by 5. $\frac{1}{5}$ of $40 = 8$

To find 3 fifths multiply by 3. $\frac{3}{5}$ of $40 = 3 \times 8$

$= 24$

1 Find

(a) $\frac{2}{5}$ of 35   (b) $\frac{5}{8}$ of 24

(c) $\frac{3}{4}$ of 36   (d) $\frac{2}{3}$ of 21

2 What volume is contained in each of these?

(a) $\frac{3}{5}$ full   (b) $\frac{2}{3}$ full   (c) $\frac{7}{10}$ full   (d) $\frac{3}{4}$ full

Find $\frac{3}{10}$ of 2 kilograms.

Change 2 kilograms to 2000 grams.

$\frac{1}{10}$ of 2000 g = 200 g

$\frac{3}{10}$ of 2000 g = 3 × 200 g

= 600 g

3 Find

(a) $\frac{2}{5}$ of 3 kilograms
(in grams)

(b) $\frac{9}{10}$ of 4 metres
(in centimetres)

(c) $\frac{3}{8}$ of £2 (in pence).

4 A $1\frac{1}{2}$ litre bottle of orange juice is $\frac{5}{6}$ full.

How many millilitres of juice are in the bottle?

Use a calculator for questions 5 to 8.

Find $\frac{3}{8}$ of 3408.   Enter   **3408.**

Press   **÷ 8 × 3 =**

to give   **1278.**

5 Find

(a) $\frac{4}{5}$ of 5875

(b) $\frac{2}{3}$ of £180 000

(c) $\frac{9}{10}$ of 360 000 m²

6 Seven-eighths of an iceberg is below the surface of the water.
An iceberg weighs 16 000 tonnes. How many tonnes of ice are

(a) above the surface   (b) below the surface?

A 9 carat gold chain weighs 36 grams. $\frac{9}{24}$ of its weight is pure gold.
The weight of pure gold = $\frac{9}{24}$ of 36 g = **13·5 grams**.

7 Use the table to calculate the weight of pure
gold in a

(a) 9 carat brooch which weighs 12 grams
(b) 18 carat chain which weighs 60 grams
(c) 22 carat bracelet which weighs 30 grams
(d) 15 carat necklace which weighs 54 grams.

	Fraction which is pure gold
22 carat	$\frac{22}{24}$
18 carat	$\frac{18}{24}$
15 carat	$\frac{15}{24}$
9 carat	$\frac{9}{24}$

8 Find the value of your own weight of 9 carat gold if pure gold costs £6 per gram.

Ask your teacher what to do next.

1 litre = 1000 ml = 1000 cm³

1 The volumes of these containers are
given in different ways.
Write each volume in another way.

(a) **45 cm³** (b) **100 ml** (c) **150 ml** (d) **175 cm³** (e) **500 ml**

2 Start a class collection of containers which have their
volumes shown. For each container, label the volume
in another way.

3 Measuring jars can have different scales.
This diagram shows part of a measuring jar.
 (a) How many small intervals are there between the
 200 ml and 300 ml marks?
 (b) What volume does each small interval represent?
 (c) What volume of liquid is shown in this jar?

4 What volume of liquid is shown in each of these jars?

(a) (b) (c) (d)

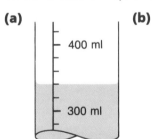 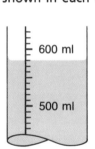 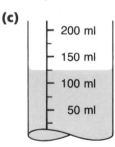 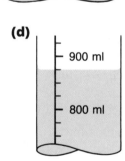

5 Do Workbook page 29.

6 When measuring the volume of liquid
in a measuring jar, make sure your **eye**
is level with the surface of the liquid.

**You need a cup, a mug and
measuring jars.**
 (a) Measure out 250 ml of water. Find
 out if this is more than, less than
 or about the same volume as, a mugful.
 (b) Measure out 180 ml of water. Find
 out if this is more than, less than
 or about the same volume as, a cupful.

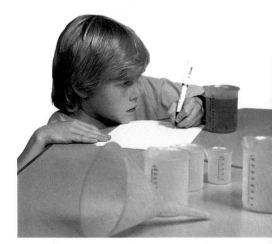

Each diagram shows part of a measuring jar.

orange juice

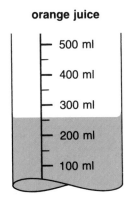

The volume of orange juice is more than 250 ml and less than 300 ml.
The volume of orange juice is **250 ml to the nearest mark**.

The volume of lime juice is more than 250 ml and less than 300 ml.
The volume of lime juice is **300 ml to the nearest mark**.

lime juice

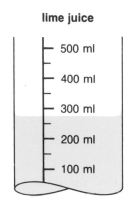

1 Read these volumes **to the nearest mark**.

(a)

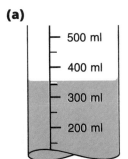

(b)

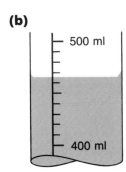

(c)

(d)

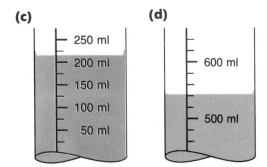

2 Work as a group.
You need measuring jars, a cup, a mug and other containers.

Estimate, then find the approximate volume of each container.
Record each volume in a table like this.

Container	My estimate	Volume
Cup		
Mug		

3 You need a clean 'medicine' bottle, a measuring jar and a label.
Stick a label like this on your bottle. ———→

Take two 5ml spoonfuls three times a day.

(a) How much 'medicine' is taken each day?
(b) How many whole days will the 'medicine' last?
   You will need to measure the volume of liquid in the full bottle.

4 For each person find how many days the medicine will last.

J.DOUGLAS
Take two
5 mL
spoonfuls
per day

250 mL

M.SULEMAN
Take one
5 ml
spoonful
three times
a day

150 ml

K. ASHWORTH
Take one
5 ml spoonful
twice per day

125 ml

You may use centimetre cubes if you wish.

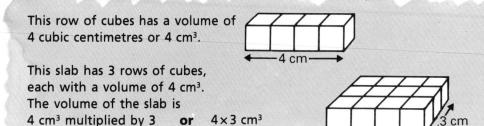

This row of cubes has a volume of 4 cubic centimetres or 4 cm³.

This slab has 3 rows of cubes, each with a volume of 4 cm³. The volume of the slab is 4 cm³ multiplied by 3   **or**   4×3 cm³

1 Find the volume in cm³ of each of these slabs.

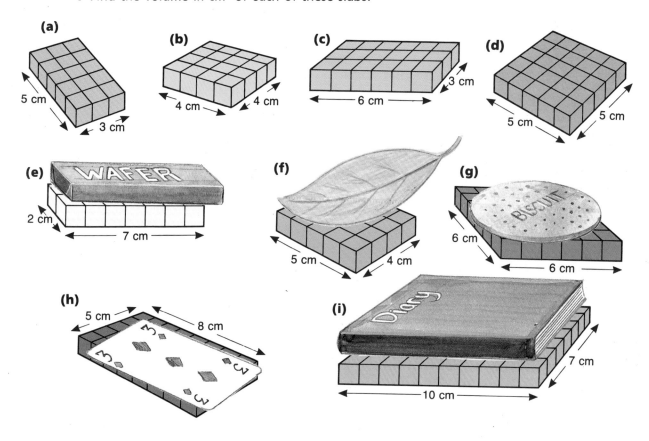

(a) 5 cm, 3 cm

(b) 4 cm, 4 cm

(c) 6 cm, 3 cm

(d) 5 cm, 5 cm

(e) WAFER, 2 cm, 7 cm

(f) 5 cm, 4 cm

(g) BISCUIT, 6 cm, 6 cm

(h) 5 cm, 8 cm

(i) Diary, 7 cm, 10 cm

2 Tony built a tanker with centimetre cubes from his construction kit.

Find the volume of
(a) the red funnel
(b) the yellow bridge
(c) the blue hull
(d) the complete tanker.

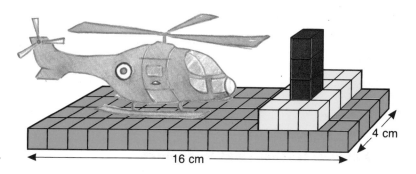

16 cm, 4 cm

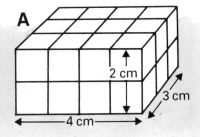

This cuboid is built with **two** layers.
The volume of one layer is
4×3 cm³
The volume of the **whole** cuboid is
4×3 cm³ multiplied by 2
or $4 \times 3 \times 2$ cm³ $= 24$ cm³

1 The cuboids **B**, **C** and **D** are built from centimetre cubes.

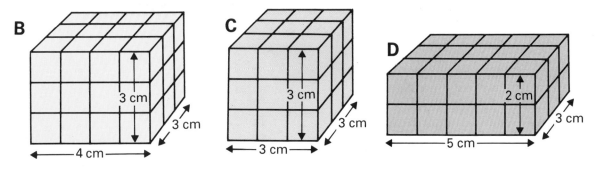

Copy and complete this table.

Cuboid	Number of cubes in a row	Number of rows	Number of layers	Volume in cm³
A	4	3	2	$4 \times 3 \times 2 = 24$
B				
C				
D				

length in cm (*l*)   breadth in cm (*b*)   height in cm (*h*)   volume in cm³ (*V*)

For every cuboid $V = l \times b \times h$

2 Find the volume in cm³ of each of these boxes.

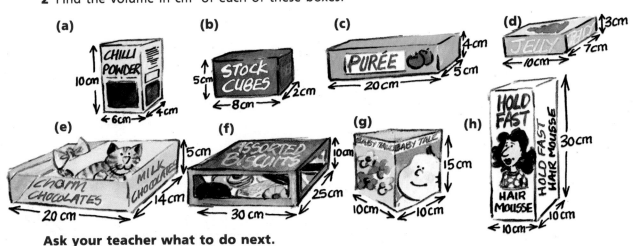

(a) CHILLI POWDER   10 cm, 6 cm, 4 cm

(b) STOCK CUBES   5 cm, 8 cm, 2 cm

(c) PURÉE   4 cm, 20 cm, 5 cm

(d) JELLY   3 cm, 10 cm, 7 cm

(e) MILK CHOCOLATES   20 cm, 14 cm

(f) ASSORTED BISCUITS   5 cm, 30 cm, 25 cm

(g) BABY TALC   10 cm, 10 cm, 10 cm

(h) HOLD FAST HAIR MOUSSE   30 cm, 15 cm, 10 cm

Ask your teacher what to do next.

Remember

100 cm = 1 m
1 centimetre is **one hundredth** of 1 metre.

1 cm = 0·01 m

1 The first arrow on this measuring tape shows 3 cm or 0·03 m.
In the same way write the length shown by each of the other arrows.

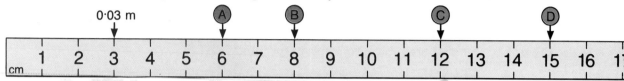

0·03 m

There are 10 mm in 1 cm and 1000 mm in 1 m.
1 millimetre is **one thousandth** of 1 metre.

1 mm = 0·001 m

2 Here is part of a metre stick marked in millimetres.

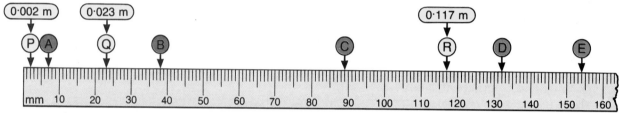

Arrow **P** shows   2 mm or   2 thousandths of a metre ⟶ 0·002 m
Arrow **Q** shows   23 mm or   23 thousandths of a metre ⟶ 0·023 m
Arrow **R** shows 117 mm or 117 thousandths of a metre ⟶ 0·117 m

Write the length shown by each of the other arrows in millimetres and as a decimal
fraction of a metre.

3 Metre sticks may be marked in millimetres as shown below. Write the length shown
by each arrow in millimetres and as a decimal fraction of a metre.

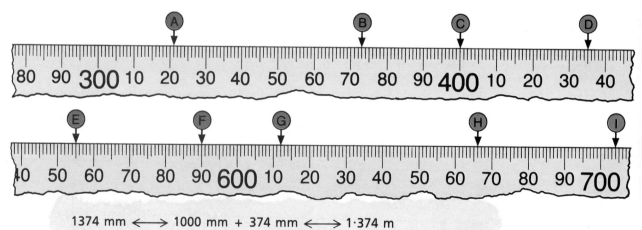

1374 mm ⟷ 1000 mm + 374 mm ⟷ 1·374 m

4 Write each of these lengths in metres:
(a) 1647 mm   (b) 1077 mm   (c) 2105 mm   (d) 1005 mm   (e) 2550 mm

5 Write each of these lengths in millimetres:
(a) 1·375 m   (b) 1·045 m   (c) 2·005 m   (d) 3·75 m   (e) 2·5 m

You may use a calculator.

1000 ml = 1 litre
1 millilitre is **one thousandth** of 1 litre.

1 ml = 0·001 litres

1 (a) Write in litres the volume of each
container.
(b) What is the total volume in litres of
three bottles of vinegar?

2 A recipe asks for 5 ml of olive oil.
Write this as a decimal fraction of a litre.

3 Write these volumes in millilitres:
(a) 1·705 litres **(b)** 0·325 litres **(c)** 0·05 litres **(d)** 1·3 litres

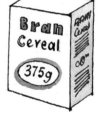

1000 g = 1 kg
1 gram is **one thousandth** of 1 kilogram.

1 g = 0·001 kg

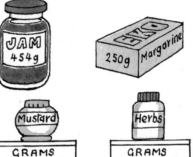

4 (a) Write in kilograms the weight of
each item shown.
(b) What is the total weight in
kilograms of all these items?

5 Write these weights in grams:
(a) 2·545 kg **(b)** 1·55 kg **(c)** 0·065 kg **(d)** 2·4 kg

6 The table below shows the weights in kilograms of four cheeses
sold by the grocer on Saturday and Sunday.
(a) Which cheese does he sell most of on Saturday?
(b) Which cheese does he sell most of on Sunday?
(c) Find the total weight of each cheese sold over the two
days.
(d) Find the difference in grams between the total weight of
Cheshire and the total weight of Edam sold over the two
days.

Name	Weight of cheese in kg	
	Saturday	Sunday
Cheshire	6·251	4·435
Brie	5·962	5·293
Edam	5·573	5·248
Stilton	5·874	5·365

4	three thousandths	two tenths	three units	one hundredth
3	two units	eight hundredths	five thousandths	four tenths
2	seven tenths	one thousandth	six tenths	eight thousandths
1	four hundredths	four units	nine hundredths	one unit
	A	**B**	**C**	**D**

Here is a number in code: **D1, A2, B3, C3**
You can find the number like this:

D1 ———→ one unit ————————————→ 1
A2 ———→ seven tenths ————————→ 0·7
B3 ———→ eight hundredths ——————→ 0·08
C3 ———→ five thousandths ————————→ 0·005
           The number is ———————→ 1·785

An Enigma machine. The Germans used these machines to code messages during the Second World War.

1 Find the number for each of these:

  (a) **D1, B4, A1, C3**   (b) **A3, C2, B3, A4**
  (c) **C4, A2, C1, B2**   (d) **B1, D3, D4, C3**
  (e) **A3, C2, B2**   (f) **D1, B3, C3**
  (g) **C4, D2**   (h) **A4**

2 Find the code for each of these numbers:

  (a) 1·691   (b) 2·783   (c) 0·215   (d) 3·403   (e) 0·008

3 The value of the arrowed numeral in **1.246** is four hundredths.

Write the value of each of these arrowed numerals:

  (a) **2.356** (b) **1.439** (c) **3.052** (d) **8.731**

  (e) **0.082** (f) **13.146** (g) **28.245** (h) **203.203**

4 Write the **greater** number in each pair:

  (a) 1·534 or 1·543   (b) 2·553 or 2·535   (c) 1·099 or 1·109
  (d) 2·110 or 2·011   (e) 0·189 or 0·198   (f) 4·199 or 4·209

5 Copy and complete each sequence:

  (a) 1·432, 1·434, 1·436, _____, _____, _____, 1·444
  (b) 0·064, 0·068, 0·072, _____, _____, _____, 0·088
  (c) 2·745, 2·740, 2·735, _____, _____, _____, 2·715

1 (a) Enter `0.345` on your calculator.

Add **one** number to make your calculator show `0.349`
Write the number you added.

Do each of these in the same way:

Enter   Make

(b) `0.421` ⟶ `0.428`

(c) `.1.526` ⟶ `1.586`

(d) `2.044` ⟶ `2.049`

2 (a) Enter `1.346` on your calculator.

Subtract **one** number to make your calculator show `1.340`
Write the number you subtracted.

Do each of these in the same way:

Enter   Make

(b) `0.747` ⟶ `0.742`

(c) `1.205` ⟶ `1.005`

(d) `3.988` ⟶ `3.938`

3 (a) Enter `2.264`

Make this number up to **5** by adding like this:

Enter ➕ ▪ ⓪ ⓪ ⑥ ✖ to add 6 thousandths ⟶ `2.27`

Enter ➕ ▪ ⓪ ③ ✖ to add 3 hundredths ⟶ `2.3`

Enter ➕ ▪ ⑦ ✖ to add 7 tenths ⟶ `3.`

Enter ➕ ② ✖ to add 2 units ⟶ `5.`

The numbers you added were   0·006, 0·03, 0·7, 2

In the same way make **5**, starting with
(b) 1·449   **(c)** 2·532   **(d)** 3·085
(e) 4·803   **(f)** 0·920   **(g)** 2·007
Write the numbers you added each time.

4 Make **10** starting with
  (a) 6·327   **(b)** 2·051   **(c)** 9·009
Write the numbers you added each time.

Ask your teacher if you can play the Calculator games.

Anton went on a Springfield cycling tour of Northern Spain. On the holiday he cycled an average distance of 30·27 km per day.

30·27 can be shown on a numberline.
It is between 30·2 and 30·3.
It is nearer **30·3**.

30·27
30·2   30·3

Anton's daily average was **30·3** km **to the nearest tenth of a kilometre** or **30·3** km **correct to the first decimal place.**

1 On a Springfield trip to the West coast of Ireland Jan cycled an average distance of 51·24 km per day.

Copy and complete:
51·24 lies between 51·2 and _____.
It is nearer _____.
Jan's daily average was _____ km to the nearest _____ of a kilometre
or _____ km correct to the _____.

51·2   51·3

2 Do Workbook page 30, question 1.

3 Write the following correct to the first decimal place:

   (a) 1·23   **(b)** 7·77   **(c)** 26·08   **(d)** 112·53
   (e) 84·03   **(f)** 0·39   **(g)** 76·92   **(h)** 4·99

You need a calculator.

4 The table shows the number of kilometres John cycled each day.

   (a) Calculate the total number of kilometres he cycled.

   (b) Check that the average distance he cycled per day was 34·18 km and write this distance correct to the first decimal place.

Mon	Tues	Wed	Thurs	Fri
26·8	34·2	32·8	29·3	47·8

5 Four women went on a week's cycling tour. For each woman in the table

   (a) calculate the total number of kilometres cycled

   (b) find the average distance cycled per day correct to the first decimal place.

	Mon	Tues	Wed	Thurs	Fri
Beth	31·2	27·2	35·1	25·5	11·7
Cara	27·3	34·6	33·2	42·4	31·1
Mandy	20·5	32·3	38·7	41·3	40·0
Vicki	45·6	48·7	65·1	52·6	52·9

6 Do Workbook page 30, questions 2 and 3.

1 Write the sizes, in right angles and in degrees, of the angles shown.

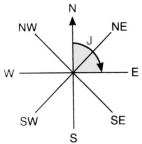 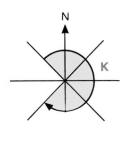 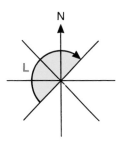 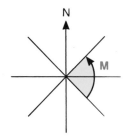

2 Each red angle is half of a right angle

$\frac{1}{2}$ **right angle = 45°**

Write the number of right angles and degrees for each coloured compass angle like this:

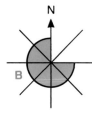

Angle	Right angles	Degrees
A	$1\frac{1}{2}$	135°

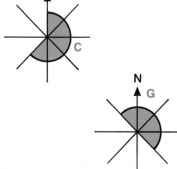

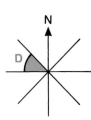 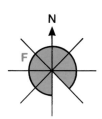

3 How many degrees does each of these angles measure:
   (a) 1 right angle   **(b)** 3 right angles   **(c)** $\frac{1}{2}$ right angle
   (d) 1 complete turn   **(e)** $2\frac{1}{2}$ right angles   **(f)** $3\frac{1}{2}$ right angles?

One complete rotation is 360°
The red angle is 360° − 240° = 120°

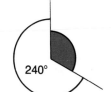

4 Calculate the size in degrees of each red angle.

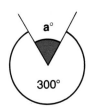 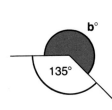 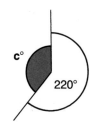 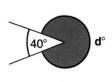 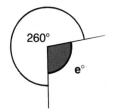

The angles used in giving directions are called **bearings**.
A bearing is measured **clockwise from North**.
The number of degrees is always given using **three figures**.

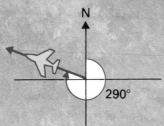

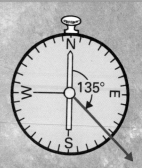

This ship is sailing on the bearing 050°

This plane is flying on the bearing 290°

The red arrow is pointing along the compass bearing 135°

1 Cut out the dotted square from **Workbook page 22**. Stick it on to a piece of cardboard. Cut out the circle. You have made a **protractor** for measuring angles.

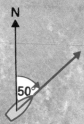

2 On the map the black dots **A** to **L** show the positions of 12 people on a treasure hunt. They are all heading for the crossroads shown by the red arrow on page 79.

Place the protractor on the first circle (**A**). Line up 000° with the North direction. Check that the bearing along which the first person **A** is heading, towards the crossroads, is 070°. Now find the other bearings **B** to **L** and record them like this: **A – 070°**

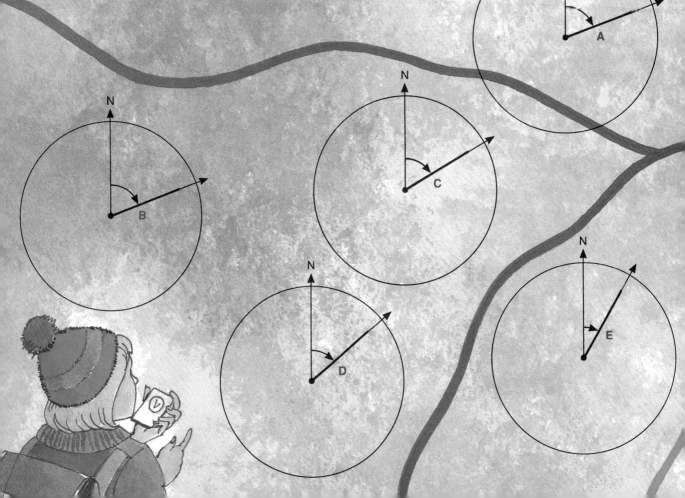

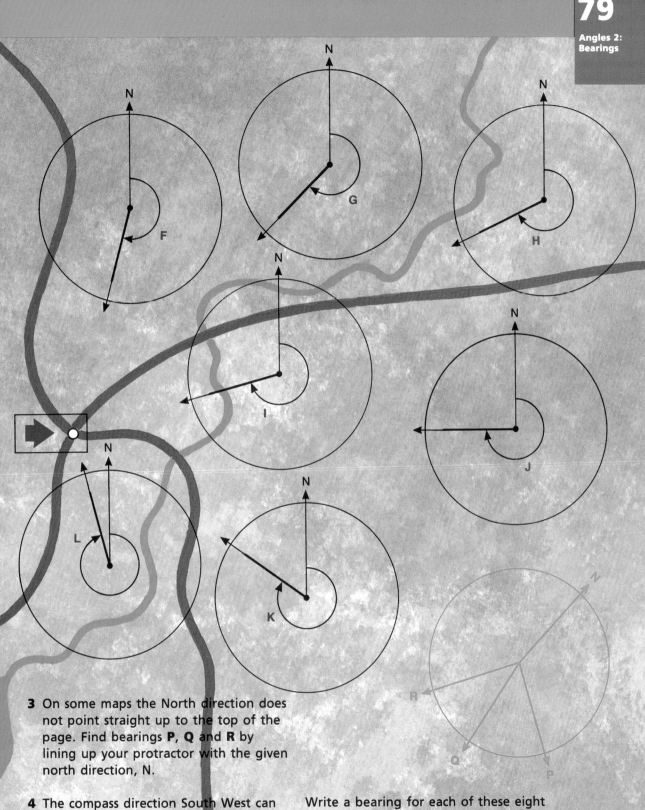

3 On some maps the North direction does
not point straight up to the top of the
page. Find bearings **P**, **Q** and **R** by
lining up your protractor with the given
north direction, N.

4 The compass direction South West can
be written as the bearing 225°.

Write a bearing for each of these eight
compass directions.

North	000°
NE	045°
. . . and so on.	

5 Do Workbook
pages 31 and 32.

Keep your protractor for Textbook page 115.

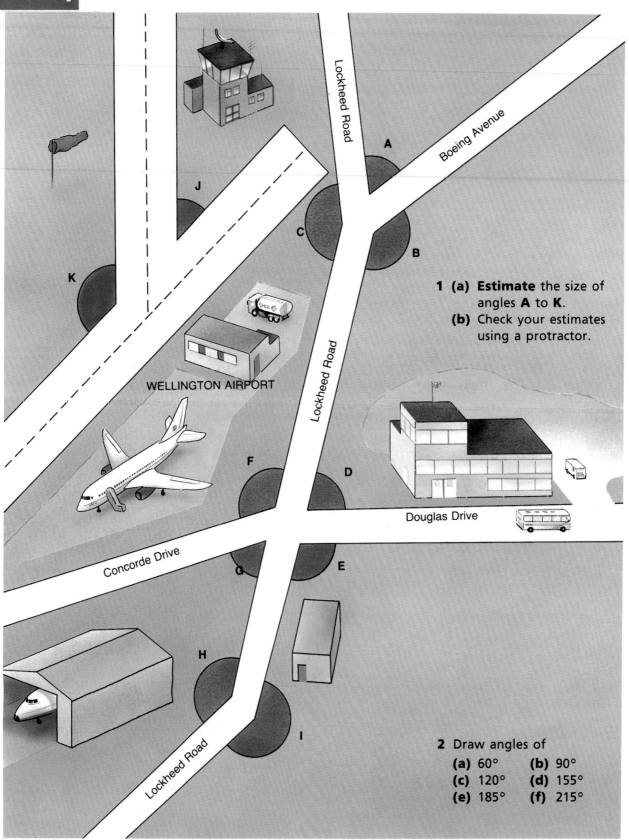

WELLINGTON AIRPORT

Lockheed Road

Boeing Avenue

Lockheed Road

Concorde Drive

Douglas Drive

Lockheed Road

1 (a) Estimate the size of
angles **A** to **K**.

(b) Check your estimates
using a protractor.

2 Draw angles of
(a) 60° (b) 90°
(c) 120° (d) 155°
(e) 185° (f) 215°

Ask your teacher what to do next.

1 Steve kept each month's *Sport* magazine over a year. He lent three copies to a friend. Which months were these?

| AUGUST | | | | | | |
Sun	Mon	Tues	Wed	Thur	Fri	Sat
			1	2	3	4
5	6	7	8	9	10	11
12	13	14	15	16	17	18
19	20	21	22	23	24	25
26	27	28	29	30	31	

SPORT JUNE 1990
SPORT MAY 1990
SPORT MARCH 1990
SPORT FEBRUARY 1990
SPORT DECEMBER 1989
SPORT NOVEMBER 1989
SPORT OCTOBER 1989
SPORT AUGUST 1989
SPORT JULY 1989

2 Use this calendar for the month of August to find the dates of
   (a) the first Friday
   (b) the second Tuesday
   (c) all the Sundays
   (d) the day one week after August 17th
   (e) the day one week before August 13th
   (f) the last weekend.

3 Write the date of the *Evening Times* for
   (a) the day after   **(b)** the day before.

No 34 647   Wednesday, October 24 1990

EVENING TIMES

4 (a) What do you think No 34 647 means?
   (b) The *Evening Times* is not published on a Sunday. Write the number and date for the following Wednesday's edition.

No 112   1 November 1990

Pop News

5 Write the date of the weekly magazine *Pop News* for   **(a)** the week after
   (b) the week before.

6 In what year do you think *Pop News* was first published? Explain your answer.

ST★RS   23 NOV 1990
ST★RS   30 NOV 1990
ST★RS   14 DEC 1990
ST★RS   21 DEC 1990
ST★RS   28 DEC 1990
ST★RS   11 JAN 1991

7 Sally began keeping the weekly magazine *Stars* from November 23rd 1990. Write the dates of the magazines which are missing from her set.

8 Beginning with next week, write dates for
   (a) six volleyball matches held weekly on Wednesdays
   (b) four discos held monthly on Fridays.

BOSTON MA 021
PM
27 OCT
1990

GLASGOW
10.10.90

COVENTRY AND WARWICKSHIRE
8 OCT
1990

AYLESBURY
17 X 90
BUCKS

PORT ELLEN
ISLE OF ISLAY
3 15 PM
13 OCT 90

9 Look at the postmarks.
   (a) List the dates in order.
   (b) Write the place of posting beside each date.

10 Make a collection of envelopes and investigate the postmarks.

Investigation

11 Do Workbook page 33.

**Time:
Durations**

Nazir and Leanne are going to Birmingham. They leave Sheffield
by bus at 16.35 and expect to arrive at Birmingham at 18.20.
They work out the journey time in different ways.

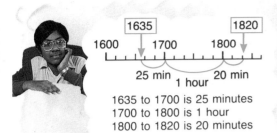

1635 → 1820

1600 1700 1800

25 min ⌣ 1 hour ⌣ 20 min

1635 to 1700 is 25 minutes
1700 to 1800 is 1 hour
1800 to 1820 is 20 minutes

The journey time is 1 hour 45 minutes.

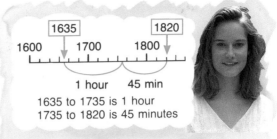

1635 → 1820

1600 1700 1800

1 hour ⌣ 45 min

1635 to 1735 is 1 hour
1735 to 1820 is 45 minutes

The journey time is 1 hour 45 minutes.

0800 0900 1000 1100 1200 1300 1400 1500 1600 1700 1800 1900 2000 2100 2200

1 Use the Edinburgh – Cardiff bus timetable and the time line.
Calculate each journey time:

(a) Edinburgh to Newcastle   (b) Newcastle to Leeds
(c) Leeds to Sheffield   (d) Leeds to Birmingham.

2 (a) Where is the longest stop?
(b) How long is it?

3 Find the time taken for each journey:

(a) Edinburgh – Birmingham   (b) Edinburgh – Leeds
(c) Leeds – Newport   (d) Newcastle – Newport
(e) Sheffield – Cardiff.

4 (a) Find the total journey time
from Edinburgh to Cardiff.
(b) How long does this bus
spend **actually travelling**?

5 Use the Aberdeen – Chester bus timetable.
Find each journey time:

(a) Aberdeen – Glasgow   (b) Preston – Warrington
(c) Lancaster – Chester   (d) Dundee – Preston.

6 On Monday the bus left Dundee on time but arrived
in Glasgow twenty minutes late.
How long did it take from Dundee to Glasgow?

7 On Thursday the bus left Glasgow twenty minutes
late but arrived in Lancaster on time.
How long did that journey take?

Ask your teacher what to do next.

EDINBURGH – CARDIFF

Edinburgh		0830
Newcastle	arr	1145
Newcastle	dep	1220
Leeds	arr	1445
Leeds	dep	1530
Sheffield		1635
Birmingham	arr	1820
Birmingham	dep	1900
Newport		2105
Cardiff		2130

ABERDEEN – CHESTER

Aberdeen		0800
Dundee		0950
Glasgow	arr	1215
Glasgow	dep	1300
Lancaster		1610
Preston	arr	1715
Preston	dep	1730
Manchester	arr	1840
Manchester	dep	1900
Warrington		1945
Chester		2020

84 Silver Star Deliveries

Detour:
Pounds/
kilograms,
Miles/
kilometres

This parcel weighs 2 lb.

Pounds is written as lb
2 pounds is written as 2 lb

2 lb is about 1 kg
1 lb is about $\frac{1}{2}$ kg

1 (a) Copy and complete the table.

(b) Use the information in your table to draw a straight-line graph on 2 mm **squared** paper.

Approximate relationship between lb and kg

Weight in lb	1	2	4	6	8	10	12
Weight in kg	0·5	1					

Use your graph.

2 Find the weight of these parcels in kilograms:

(a) 3 lb

(b) 7 lb

(c) 9 lb

(d) 6½ lb

3 Find the weight of these parcels in pounds:

(a) 2·5 kg

(b) 5·5 kg

(c) 1·25 kg

(d) 9·75 kg

Weight in kg (vertical axis, values 0, 0.5, 1, 1.5, 2, 2.5, 3)
Weight in lb (horizontal axis, values 0, 1, 2, 3)

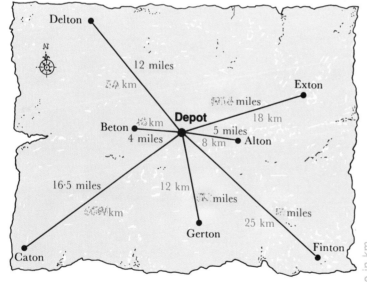

Delton
12 miles
?? km
Exton
??? miles
Depot
18 km
Beton
?? km
5 miles
4 miles
8 km Alton
16·5 miles
12 km
??? km
? miles
? miles
25 km
Caton
Gerton
Finton

The map shows the approximate distances, marked in both miles and kilometres, of some towns from the Silver Star depot. Some of the markings are unclear. Alton is about **5 miles** or **8 kilometres** from the depot.

5 miles is about 8 km
1 mile is about 1·6 km

4 (a) Copy and complete the table.

Approximate relationship between miles and km

Distance in miles	5	10	15	20
Distance in km	8			

(b) Use the information in your table to draw a straight-line graph on 2 mm squared paper.

Distance in km (vertical axis, values 10, 20)
Distance in miles (horizontal axis, values 5, 10, 15)

5 Use your graph.
Give the distance in **both** miles and kilometres from the Silver Star depot to each town.

Ask your teacher what to do next.

1 Copy and complete using either **more likely** or **less likely**.

(a) It is _____ to rain in London than the Sahara Desert.

(b) A film shown on TV is _____ to be in black and white than in colour.

(c) Picnicking in summer is _____ than picnicking in winter.

(d) A postman is _____ to deliver mail in the morning than in the evening.

2 Dropping the card.

You need two playing cards.
Work with a partner.

Marion is trying to drop a playing card so that it lands touching the card on the floor.

(a) Which do you think is more likely?
  • The cards will touch.
  • The cards will not touch.

(b) Each of you should try Marion's experiment 20 times. Your partner can record your results on **Workbook page 34**.

3 Dropping the coin.

On plain paper draw a square grid with the sizes shown.

You need a 1p coin.
Work with a partner.

Asif drops a 1p coin on this grid from a height of about 15 cm.
He tries to land it on the centre square.

(a) Which do you think is least likely?
  • The coin will land in a square.
  • The coin will land on a line.
  • The coin will land outside the grid.

(b) Each of you should try Asif's experiment 20 times.
Your partner can record your results on **Workbook page 34**.

3 cm

← 3 cm →

4 Copy and complete using either **impossible** or **certain**.

(a) It is _____ that you will live forever.

(b) It is _____ that it will become dark tonight.

(c) If you take a bath it is _____ that you will get wet.

(d) It is _____ that you can be in two places at the same time.

Do you ever play card games? A pack of standard playing cards has four **suits**. Each suit has 13 cards.

1 Are you a mind reader? . . . Find out by doing **Workbook page 34**. **You need a pack of playing cards. Work with a partner.**

2 You need a die and a bag containing a red and a green counter.

(a) Roll the die and pick one of the counters from the bag. Record the **outcome** in a table like this.

Number on die	Colour of counter
3	Green

Repeat 10 times.

(b) Compare results with your partner.
- Are your outcomes the same?
- Are **any** of your outcomes the same?
- Do you have outcomes your partner does **not** have?

(c) Make a list of the outcomes you did **not** have in your experiment.

3 Angela makes a square spinner. She spins it and then tosses a coin. The outcome shown can be written as (2, T) where T stands for a tail.

List all the possible outcomes in the same way.

4 Steve throws a die which has two red faces, two blue faces and two green faces. Then he tosses a coin. The outcome shown can be written as (Red, H).

List all the possible outcomes in the same way.

5 Lisa puts three cards with the letters A, B and C into a bag.

She takes out two of the cards **at random** from the bag.
The outcome shown can be written as (A, B).

List all the possible outcomes in the same way.

6 Toss a 2p coin and then toss a 5p coin. List all the possible outcomes.

When a coin is tossed
- 'showing a head' is as **equally likely** as 'showing a tail'
- there is an **even chance** or a 1 in 2 chance of 'showing a head'
- the **probability** of 'showing a head' is **1 in 2**.

1 Lynn marks one side of a counter **X** and the other side ✔.
She spins the counter. Write **true** or **false** for each of the
following:
  (a) The number of possible outcomes is 2.
  (b) The counter is as equally likely to land showing **X** as
     showing ✔.
  (c) ✔ has an even chance of showing.
  (d) **X** does **not** have a 1 in 2 chance of showing.
  (e) The probability of showing ✔ is 1 in 2.

2 What is the probability of showing **X** ?

3 Gaz makes a square spinner like the one shown here.
  (a) List the 4 possible outcomes he can get if he spins it.
  (b) In how many ways • can red occur • can green occur?
  (c) Is red as equally likely to occur as green?
  (d) What is the probability that • red occurs • green occurs?

4 Marcia the Magnifico has 7 rabbit cards and 10 dove cards in
a top hat.
How many rabbit cards should be added to the hat so that
the probability of Marcia picking a rabbit card is 1 in 2?

On this **probability scale**, a probability of **1 in 2** is written as $\frac{1}{2}$.

0	$\frac{1}{2}$	1
impossible	evens	certain

5 Choose words **and** numbers from the probability scale to answer the questions.

A tube contains 10 brown and 10 yellow Smarties. A Smartie is picked at random.
What is the probability of picking
  (a) a brown Smartie   **(b)** a yellow Smartie   **(c)** a red Smartie   **(d)** a Smartie?

Choose from **0**, **less than** $\frac{1}{2}$, $\frac{1}{2}$, **greater than** $\frac{1}{2}$, or **1** to answer questions **6** and **7**.

6 Tracy has a set of 10 cards which she shuffles. Five cards show a Renault, 4 a Metro,
and 1 a BMW. If Tracy picks a card at random what is the probability of her picking
  (a) a Renault   **(b)** a Metro   **(c)** a BMW   **(d)** a bicycle   **(e)** a car?

7 There are 7 red, 1 white and 2 green cars on Tracy's cards.
What is the probability of her picking
  (a) a red car   **(b)** a green car   **(c)** a white car?

Ask your teacher what to do next.

1 (a) Copy this pattern.

(b) What do you **think** the total for row 5 will be? Check your answer.

(c) Which row do you **think** will total 36? Check.

row total

			1						1
		1	2	1					4
	1	2	3	2	1				9
1	2	3	4	3	2	1			16

row 1 ⟶
row 2 ⟶
row 3 ⟶
row 4 ⟶
row 5 ⟶

2 You need newspapers.

Choose a newspaper with double page sheets **only**.

Spread out any double page sheet.

(a) Add the page numbers on the front.

(b) Add the page numbers on the back.

(c) Compare each total with the number of pages in the whole newspaper. What do you notice?

(d)

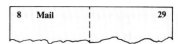

These are sheets from the *News*, the *Post* and the *Mail*. How many pages altogether has each newspaper?

3 (a) Use sticks or straws of equal length to make these three 'L' patterns.

(b) Now make the next two patterns.

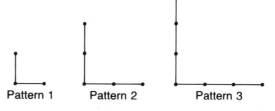

Pattern 1   Pattern 2   Pattern 3

(c) Copy and complete this table for the patterns.

Pattern number	1	2	3	4	5
Number of sticks					

(d) How many sticks or straws would there be
• in the tenth pattern
• in the fiftieth pattern?

4 (a) Use sticks or another material to make a series of patterns of your own. Describe your pattern in words.

(b) Repeat using another material.

These five schools are members of a school swimming league. Each team has to play **one** match against each of the others.

1 (a) How many matches has each team to play?
(b) Using letters, list all the matches which have to be played. Write **H v G** for Hillgrange **v** Gladeside, and so on.
(c) How many matches are to be played altogether?

2 The table shows the number of matches each team had played by 7th March and by 14th March.
(a) Which team had played all its matches by 7th March?
(b) Which match took place between the 7th and 14th March?
(c) Which matches still have to be played after 14th March?

Team	Numbers of matches played	
	by 7th March	by 14th March
Hillgrange	3	3
Gladeside	3	4
Learnwell	2	2
Derwent	4	4
Woodvale	2	3

3 The four members of the Derwent relay team are Amy, Brenda, Carol and Dianne.
Dianne must always swim last because she's the fastest, but the others can swim in any order.
List all the possible orders in which the team can swim.

There are six races in the match between Hillgrange and Gladeside.
In each race there are four swimmers, two from each school.
Points are awarded for each race as shown in the table.

Place	Points
1st	5
2nd	2
3rd	1

4 In each **race**, what is
(a) the greatest　**(b)** the least number of points that can be scored by one school?

5 Gladeside scored 20 points altogether, 7 of their swimmers scoring the points. A third place was gained by 3 of the swimmers. How many Gladeside swimmers gained　**(a)** a first place　**(b)** a second place?

Challenge

6 How many points did Hillgrange score in the match?

Ask your teacher what to do next.

Work in a group.

**1 You need marbles, six 36 cm strips
of card and sticky tape.**

(a) Fold one card strip to make a
triangular shape. Join its ends
without overlapping.

(b) Fill the triangular shape with **one
layer** of marbles. How many
marbles are needed?

(c) Fold each of the other card strips
to make a different shape. Find
which shape holds most marbles in
one layer.

**2 You need notepaper,
envelopes, card,
scissors and glue.**

The notepaper and
envelopes are a present
for a friend.
Make an attractive
folder to hold them.

**3 You need a ball, card,
scissors and sticky tape.**

Make a closed box
which is just large
enough to hold the ball.

**4 You need one sheet
of card about the
same size as this
page, about 500 cm³
of sand, scissors and
sticky tape.**

Make an open-top
container which is just
large enough to hold all
the sand.

Ask your teacher what to do next.

Did you know that the oceans and seas
cover about 71% of the Earth's surface?
Rivers and lakes cover about another 3%.

Percentages are fractions with denominator 100.

15 out of 100

15% means

$\frac{15}{100}$

100% means

100 out of 100

$\frac{100}{100}$

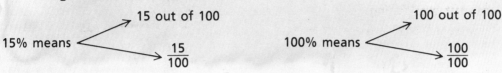

1 This rectangle is divided
into 100 equal parts.

What percentage of the rectangle is **(a)** red **(b)** blue **(c)** white?

2 Each of these **(a)**
diagrams is
divided into
100 equal parts.

(b)

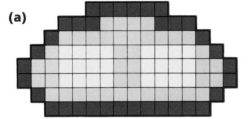 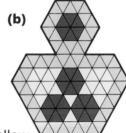

For each diagram find the percentage coloured red, blue, and yellow.

3 Do Workbook page 35, question 1.

100% of something means the whole of it.

4 (a) 75% of Tom's garden is grass. What percentage is **not** grass?
   (b) 20% of his apple crop is not fit for sale.
       What percentage of the crop is fit for sale?
   (c) Tom made compost using peat and sand.
       His compost was 60% peat. What percentage was sand?

$20\% = \frac{20}{100} = \frac{1}{5}$

5 In the same way, write as a fraction
   (a) 10% **(b)** 50% **(c)** 25%
   (d) 1%   **(e)** 75% **(f)** 100%

 Remember

$1\% = \frac{1}{100}$ $10\% = \frac{1}{10}$ $20\% = \frac{1}{5}$ $25\% = \frac{1}{4}$ $50\% = \frac{1}{2}$ $75\% = \frac{3}{4}$

20% of $15 = \frac{1}{5}$ of $15 = 3$

6 In the same way, find:
   (a) 10% of 60   **(b)** 50% of 18   **(c)** 20% of 45
   (d) 25% of 28   **(e)** 1% of 200   **(f)** 75% of 40

7 Which is greater, 25% of £5·24 *or* 20% of £6·50?

8 Do Workbook page 35, questions 3 and 4.

Strolon is a grim, grey planet! It is ruled by unjust and greedy senators. Their deputies use soldiers to keep the workers in order.

20% of 85 = $\frac{1}{5}$ of 85 = 17

$$\overset{17}{5\overline{)8^35}}$$

1 Find

(a) 10% of 150 (b) 50% of 592 (c) 25% of 208 (d) 20% of 305

2 The population of Strolon is 90 million.
    50% are ruling senators
    20% are deputies
    10% are soldiers
and the rest are workers.

How many of each are there?

Find 30% of 410.   10% of 410 = 41
                    30% of 410 = 123 (3 × 10%)

3 In the same way find

(a) 40% of 240   (b) 60% of 130   (c) 90% of 820

4 The total farm land on Strolon is 280 million hectares. Of this land,
    40% is used for growing corn
    30% for growing oats
    20% for rearing cattle
and 10% for rearing sheep.

Find how much land is used for each.

Find 15% of 260.   10% of 260 = 26
                    5% of 260 = 13 ($\frac{1}{2}$ of 10%)
                   15% of 260 = 39

5 In the same way find 15% of

(a) 840   (b) 620   (c) 9940   (d) 7020

6 In Strolon, 20 000 workers are employed in the infamous zinc mines. The senators decide to move 15% of these workers to farm work. How many do they move?

Remember

$\frac{29}{100}$ or **29 hundredths** can be written as **29%**

1

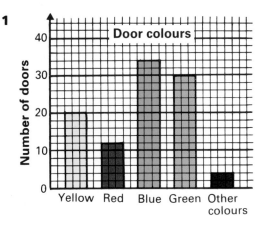

Door colours — bar graph: Number of doors vs Yellow, Red, Blue, Green, Other colours

The bar graph shows the colour of 100 doors in Poll Street.

20 of the 100 doors are yellow.

$\frac{20}{100}$ (**20 hundredths**) or **20%** of the doors are yellow.

What percentage of the doors are
(a) red   **(b)** blue
(c) green   **(d)** other colours?

2 Go to **Workbook page 36**, and show in circle **1** the information about the doors.

3 A survey of 25 pupils was made to see what type of footwear they wore.

10 out of the 25 wore trainers.
$\frac{10}{25} = \frac{40}{100}$ (40 hundredths)
40% wore trainers.

What percentage of the pupils wore
(a) boots   **(b)** shoes   **(c)** other types of footwear?

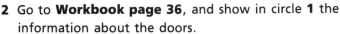

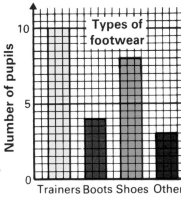

Types of footwear — bar graph: Number of pupils vs Trainers, Boots, Shoes, Other types

4 Go to **Workbook page 36**, and show in circle **2** the information about the footwear.

5 (a) Carry out your own survey of 25 pupils to find what type of footwear they wear.
Express your survey results as percentages.
(b) Go to **Workbook page 36**, and show in circle **3** this information.

6 (a) In a class of 20 pupils, 16 had a calculator.
What percentage of the class had a calculator?
(b) Carry out a survey of 20 pupils in your class or school and find what percentage have a calculator.

7 In a fish tank there were 27 neon tetras, 15 angel fish and 8 guppies.
What percentage of the fish were
(a) neon tetras   **(b)** angel fish   **(c)** guppies?

8 Go to **Workbook page 36**, and show in circle **4** the information about the fish.

35% means 35 hundredths
So 35% = 0·35

5% means 5 hundredths
So 5% = 0·05

1 Write each percentage as a decimal fraction.

(a) 45%   (b) 57%   (c) 15%   (d) 22%
(e) 84%   (f) 66%   (g) 9%   (h) 30%
(i) 7%   (j) 20%   (k) 1%   (l) 90%

Use a calculator.

About 8% of all students are left handed. In the first year at Moorcroft College there are 225 students. About how many would you expect to be left handed?

To find 8% of 225,

Enter `0.08` Press ✕ 2 2 5 = to give `18.`

You would expect about **18 students** to be left handed.

2 Find

(a) 8% of 775   (b) 6% of 350   (c) 12% of 3225
(d) 15% of 580   (e) 24% of £625   (f) 88% of £2250
(g) 55% of £440   (h) 96% of 925   (i) 48% of £1500

3 At Moorcroft College there are 575 students altogether.
• 92% **are** right handed   • 44% are male
• 12% wear glasses   • 96% have fillings in their teeth.

How many students

(a) are right handed   (b) wear glasses
(c) do not wear glasses   (d) are female
(e) have **no** fillings in their teeth?

Jim is the college gardener.

The area of the garden is 1·5 hectares (15 000 m²).
47% of the area is flower beds, 26% vegetable plots, 9% paths, and 18% lawns.

4 Find the area of each part of the garden in square metres.

LAWN SAND
85% Silver sand
10% sulphate of ammonia
5% sulphate of iron

5 To treat the lawns, Jim has to spread 100 g of lawn sand on each square metre.
How many kilograms of lawn sand does he need?

6 Jim makes his own lawn sand using the recipe shown. How many kilograms of each material does he need to treat the lawns?

Ask your teacher what to do next.

You need a calculator.

You can check multiplication
by doing two divisions.

$$43 \times 8 = 344$$

(check)

$$344 \div 8 = 43$$ $$344 \div 43 = 8$$

You can check division by
doing two multiplications.

$$377 \div 13 = 29$$

(check)

$$29 \times 13 = 377$$ $$13 \times 29 = 377$$

1 For each of the following, do the multiplication and check it
by doing **two divisions**:
(a) 9×18 **(b)** 17×22 **(c)** 23×28 **(d)** 56×11 **(e)** 13×32

2 Do **one division** to check which of these are true:
(a) $8 \times 19 = 152$ **(b)** $7 \times 23 = 151$ **(c)** $11 \times 25 = 275$
(d) $17 \times 22 = 374$ **(e)** $21 \times 31 = 641$ **(f)** $27 \times 46 = 1442$

3 John did these six divisions. Use only the number keys and
[×] [=] to find which calculations he had correct.

> (a) $135 \div 9 = 15$ (b) $527 \div 17 = 31$ (c) $441 \div 21 = 21$
>
> (d) $986 \div 29 = 34$ (e) $775 \div 31 = 35$ (f) $1089 \div 33 = 43$

4 Use only the number keys and [×] [=] for these problems:

(a) A double decker bus
holds 43 passengers.
How many buses are
needed for 301
passengers?

(b) A lift holds 18 people.
How many times will it
be needed to take 162
people to the 6th floor?

(c) 24 people share the
first prize of £600 in
the football pools.
How much does each
receive?

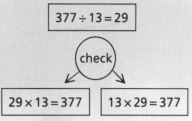

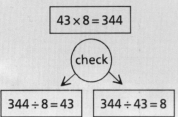

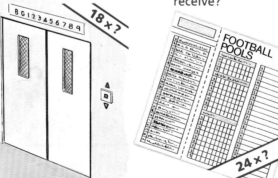

(d) There are 176 guests at
Angela and Jim's wedding.
Each table can seat 14
people. How many tables
do they need?

Ask your teacher what to do next.

You can find the answer to 3×28 mentally like this:

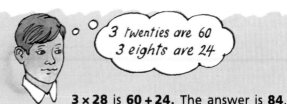

3 twenties are 60
3 eights are 24

3×28 is **60 + 24**. The answer is **84**.

1 Find each answer mentally:
(a) 2×43 (b) 3×32 (c) 3×24 (d) 4×23
(e) 54×2 (f) 56×4 (g) 48×3 (h) 37×3

Wholesome Foods deliver their tins of soup in boxes of 24.
How many tins are there altogether in 30 boxes?

The total number of tins is **30 × 24**
This can be found by $3 \times 24 \rightarrow 72$
$10 \times 72 \rightarrow 720$
The total number of tins is **720**.

2 Find each answer mentally: (a) 20×31 (b) 40×22 (c) 33×30 (d) 40×17
(e) 48×20 (f) 40×24 (g) 30×26 (h) 58×30

3 A carton of mineral water holds 18 bottles.
How many bottles are there altogether in
(a) 20 cartons (b) 40 cartons (c) 60 cartons?

Multiplying by 50

To find 27×50: **multiply 27 by 100** to give 2700,
then **divide by 2** to give **1350.**

$27 \times 100 \longrightarrow 2700$, then $2700 \div 2 \longrightarrow 1350$

4 Find each answer mentally: (a) 24×50 (b) 50×29 (c) 43×50 (d) 50×34
(e) 76×50 (f) 50×35 (g) 18×50 (h) 50×17

5 A box contains 36 ice cream cones. How many cones
are there altogether in 50 boxes?

Bags of *Wholesome* crisps are packed in boxes of 48.
How many bags are there in 200 boxes?

The total number of bags is **200 × 48.** This can be found by $2 \times 48 \rightarrow 96$
$100 \times 96 \rightarrow 9600$
There are **9600** bags altogether.

6 Find (a) 300×21 (b) 200×42 (c) 27×200 (d) 400×23
(e) 43×300 (f) 59×200 (g) 400×36 (h) 38×300

7 A row of knitting has 64 stitches. How many stitches are there in 200 rows?

Sandra's shop sells Christmas crackers.
A large Christmas cracker costs her £1·05.
What is the cost of 100 crackers?

100 crackers cost **£1·05 × 100 → £105**

Remember

To multiply by 100: move each digit **two** places to the left.
With money, pence become pounds.

1 Find mentally **(a)** £2·64 × 100 **(b)** 100 × £1·49 **(c)** 58p × 100
(d) 100 × £7·32 **(e)** 100 × £4·99 **(f)** £17·25 × 100
(g) 100 × £8·50 **(h)** £19·05 × 100

Sandra orders 200 boxes of Christmas crackers at £2·34 per box.
What is the total cost of the crackers?

The total cost is **200 × £2·34**
This can be found by **100 × £2·34 → £234**
2 × £234 → £468

2 Find **(a)** 200 × £1·42 **(b)** 300 × £3·23 **(c)** £2·06 × 400 **(d)** 200 × £3·54
(e) 300 × £4·32 **(f)** £1·19 × 400 **(g)** 300 × £4·15 **(h)** £2·25 × 400

3 A children's charity buys 200 jigsaw puzzles from Sandra's shop.
Each puzzle costs £3·75. What is the cost of the 200 puzzles?

There are 20 Christmas
tree lights in a set.
How many sets can be
made from 2560 lights?

The number of sets is **2560 ÷ 20**
This can be found by **2560 ÷ 2 → 1280**
1280 ÷ 10 → 128
The number of sets is **128**.

4 Find **(a)** 2780 ÷ 20 **(b)** 3570 ÷ 30 **(c)** 4520 ÷ 40 **(d)** 4320 ÷ 20
(e) 5840 ÷ 40 **(f)** 5720 ÷ 20 **(g)** 2850 ÷ 30 **(h)** 6720 ÷ 40

Remember

To divide by 100: move each digit **two** places to the right.
With money, pounds become pence.

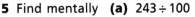

5 Find mentally **(a)** 243 ÷ 100 **(b)** 568 ÷ 100 **(c)** 1675 ÷ 100 **(d)** 480 ÷ 100
(e) £368 ÷ 100 **(f)** £475 ÷ 100 **(g)** £750 ÷ 100 **(h)** £95 ÷ 100

Sandra pays £546 for 300 boxes of
Christmas decorations. Find the cost
of one box of decorations.

The cost of one box is **£546 ÷ 300**
This can be found by **£546 ÷ 3 → £182**
£182 ÷ 100 → £1·82

6 Find **(a)** £248 ÷ 200 **(b)** £519 ÷ 300 **(c)** £856 ÷ 400 **(d)** £372 ÷ 200

Ask your teacher what to do next.

Work with a partner.

1 (a) Count how many times you can sign your autograph in 1 minute.

(b) Record: **My autograph rate is _____ times per minute.**

2 (a) Find out how to measure someone's pulse beat. Count how often each other's pulse beats in 30 seconds.

(b) Calculate how often your own pulse beats in 1 minute.

(c) Record: **My pulse rate is _____ beats per minute.**

3

Amin	Barbara	Carol
Blinked 5 times in 20 seconds	Blinked 7 times in ½ minute	Blinked twice in 10 seconds

(a) Calculate the blink rate **per minute** for each pupil.

(b) Find and record your own blink rate per minute.

(c) Put the **four** blink rates in order starting with the slowest.

Angela Newman earned £900 for a 6 minute singing spot!

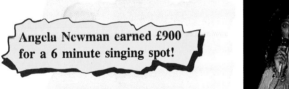

In **1 minute** Angela earned
£900 ÷ 6 = £150
Her earning rate was
£150 per minute.

4 Find

(a) Typing rate in words per minute.

(b) Joining rate in handles per minute.

(c) Packing rate in boxes per minute.

In 5 minutes Doreen typed 300 words

Marg joined handles on to 48 cups in 3 minutes.

machine packed 28 boxes in 2 minutes.

(d) Knitting rate in stitches per minute.

(e) Wingbeat rate in beats per minute.

(f) Bricklaying rate in bricks per minute.

Mrs Jones knitted 800 stitches in 10 minutes.

A humming bird beat its wings 9600 times in 2 minutes.

Steve Mason laid 240 bricks in 20 minutes.

There are 60 seconds in a minute. Not much can happen in a second . . . or can it? You can find out by doing this page.

Work as a group of three. You need a long measuring tape and a timer.

1 (a) Find how many metres each of you walks in 10 seconds.
  (b) Record:
      In **1 second** I walk about _____ metres.
      My walking rate is _____ metres per second.

2 Repeat question **1** for running.

3 Find

  (a) Wingbeat rate in beats per second.

  (b) Dive rate in metres per second.

  (c) Travel rate in metres per second.

The wings of a swallowtail butterfly beat 50 times in 10 seconds.

A falcon can dive 150 metres in 5 seconds.

The black mamba snake ... 24 metres in ... seconds.

4 Calculate and record how many metres each animal travelled in 1 second. Use a calculator if you wish.

(a) A cheetah ran 75 metres in 3 seconds.

(b) A racehorse ran 600 metres in 30 seconds.

(c) A greyhound ran 425 metres in 25 seconds.

  (d) An antelope ran 150 metres in 10 seconds.

  (e) A sea-lion swam 150 metres in 15 seconds.

A sea-lion swims 10 metres in 1 second.
We say its **speed** is **10 metres per second** or 10 m/s.

5 Write the speed of each animal in question **4** like this:
    Speed of sea-lion is 10 metres per second.

Eric ran 1500 metres in 4 minutes 12 seconds.
4 minutes 12 seconds is 252 seconds.

In **1 second** he ran 1500÷252→ `5.9523809` metres.
His running speed was about **6 metres per second**.

1 Find each speed in metres per second to the nearest whole number.

(a) Carl ran 200 metres
in 24 seconds.

(b) Donna ran 400 metres
in 65 seconds.

(c) Lisa ran 100 metres
in 14 seconds.

(d) Dick cycled 500 metres
in 30 seconds.

(e) Evelyn swam 100 metres
in 58 seconds.

(f) Frank rowed 2000 metres
in 8 minutes 25 seconds.

A Boeing 747 flew 5600 kilometres in 8 hours.
In **1 hour** it flew 5600÷8=700 kilometres.
Its speed was **700 kilometres per hour**.

2 Find each speed in kilometres per hour to the nearest whole number.

(a) 5400 km in 9 hours

(b) 868 km in 7 hours

(c) 1008 km in 24 hours

(d) 402 km in 6 hours

(e) 816 km in 12 hours

(f) 384 km in 8 hours

(g) Helicopter → 495 km in 4 hours

(h) Bicycle → 125 km in 6 hours

(i) Power boat → 483 km in 8 hours

(j) Yacht → 55 km in 3 hours.

3 Do Workbook pages 40 and 41.

The average temperature in Britain in the summer at midday is
about 21°C . . . but temperatures vary all over the world at
different times of the year.

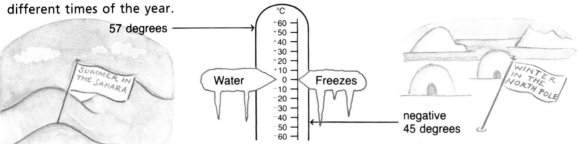

57 degrees

°C
+60
+50
+40
+30
+20
+10
0   Water   Freezes
-10
-20
-30
-40 negative
-50 45 degrees
-60

Temperatures can be recorded in different ways.

57 degrees **above** freezing → **positive** 57° Celsius → +57°C
45 degrees **below** freezing → **negative** 45° Celsius → ‾45°C

1 Record each temperature in three ways.

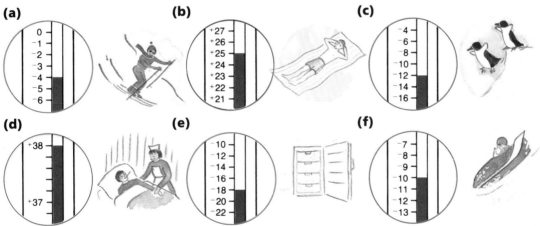

(a) 0 -1 -2 -3 -4 -5 -6

(b) +27 +26 +25 +24 +23 +22 +21

(c) -4 -6 -8 -10 -12 -14 -16

(d) +38 +37

(e) -10 -12 -14 -16 -18 -20 -22

(f) -7 -8 -9 -10 -11 -12 -13

2 Write each temperature in two other ways.
  (a) 1 degree below freezing   **(b)** +7° Celsius
  (c) 12 degrees below freezing **(d)** 18 degrees above freezing
  (e) ‾18°C   **(f)** negative 11°C

3 Record each height and depth in two ways.

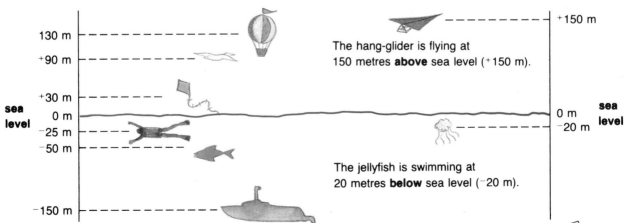

+150 m

130 m
+90 m

The hang-glider is flying at
150 metres **above** sea level (+150 m).

+30 m
sea level 0 m
-25 m
-50 m

0 m sea level
-20 m

The jellyfish is swimming at
20 metres **below** sea level (‾20 m).

-150 m

4 Go to Workbook page 39.

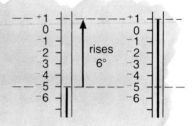

FREDDY'S FROZEN FOOD

Freddy's Frozen Foods factory has a large thermometer outside the building to show people the temperature.

1 Which is hotter   **(a)** ⁺4°C or ⁺9°C
(b) ⁻5°C or 0°C   **(c)** ⁺2°C or ⁻7°C?

2 Which is colder   **(a)** ⁺1°C or ⁺7°C
(b) ⁺3°C or ⁻5°C   **(c)** ⁻1°C or ⁻6°C?

If the temperature starts at ⁻5°C,
and rises by 6 degrees,
the thermometer will show ⁺1°C.

rises 6°

3 What will the thermometer show if the temperature starts at
(a) ⁺2°C and rises by 5 degrees
(b) ⁻2°C and rises by 7 degrees
(c) ⁻4°C and rises by 4 degrees?

4 By how many degrees does the temperature **rise** when it goes from
(a) ⁺7°C to ⁺11°C   **(b)** ⁻3°C to ⁺2°C
(c) ⁻6°C to 0°C   **(d)** ⁻5°C to ⁻1°C?

5 What will the thermometer show if the temperature starts at
(a) ⁺6°C and falls by 3 degrees
(b) ⁺3°C and falls by 5 degrees?

6 By how many degrees does the temperature **fall** when it goes from
(a) ⁺5°C to ⁺2°C   **(b)** 0°C to ⁻6°C
(c) ⁻4°C to ⁻7°C   **(d)** ⁺10°C to ⁻5°C?

7 At what floor will the lift
stop if it starts at
(a) floor ⁺1 and goes up 4 floors
(b) floor ⁻3 and goes up 3 floors
(c) floor ⁻2 and goes up 5 floors?

8 At what floor will the lift
stop if it starts at
(a) floor ⁺2 and goes down 5 floors
(b) floor 0 and goes down 2 floors
(c) floor ⁻1 and goes down 3 floors?

9 How many floors does the lift
go up if it goes from
(a) floor ⁺2 to floor ⁺5
(b) floor ⁻4 to floor ⁻2
(c) floor ⁻3 to floor ⁺5?

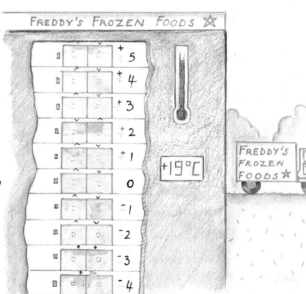

Each chest freezer at the factory has a thermometer which is
used to check the temperature.

⁻20 ⁻19 ⁻18 ⁻17 ⁻16 ⁻15 ⁻14 ⁻13 ⁻12 ⁻11 ⁻10 ⁻9 ⁻8 ⁻7 ⁻6 ⁻5 ⁻4 ⁻3 ⁻2 ⁻1 0 ⁺1 ⁺2 ⁺3 ⁺4 ⁺5 ⁺6 ⁺7 ⁺8 ⁺9 ⁺10 ⁺11 ⁺12

1 What will the thermometer show if the temperature starts at
   (a) ⁻6°C and rises by 4 degrees
   (b) 0°C and falls by 12 degrees
   (c) ⁻15°C and rises by 11 degrees
   (d) ⁺11°C and falls by 19 degrees?

The freezers at Freddy's work best at ⁻18°C.

To reach ⁻18°C,
the temperature of this
freezer will have to
rise by 2 degrees.

⁻21 ⁻20 ⁻19 ⁻18 ⁻17 ⁻16

To reach ⁻18°C,
the temperature of this
freezer will have to
drop by 4 degrees.

⁻18 ⁻17 ⁻16 ⁻15 ⁻14 ⁻13

2 For each freezer, give the drop or rise in temperature needed
   to reach ⁻18°C.

(a)

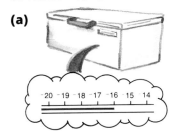

⁻20 ⁻19 ⁻18 ⁻17 ⁻16 ⁻15 ⁻14

(b)

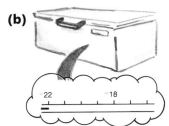

⁻22   ⁻18

(c)

⁻16 ⁻15 ⁻14 ⁻13 ⁻12 ⁻11 ⁻10

Dave Bartlett manages the quick chill store.
He operates a booster lever to speed up the
freezing process.

FREEZE   DEFROST
⁻10 ⁻9 ⁻8 ⁻7 ⁻6 ⁻5 ⁻4 ⁻3 ⁻2 ⁻1 0 ⁺1 ⁺2 ⁺3 ⁺4 ⁺5 ⁺6 ⁺7 ⁺8 ⁺9 ⁺10

3 What would be the reading on the scale if the lever started at
   (a) ⁻2 and increased by 5   **(b)** 0 and decreased by 2
   (c) ⁻4 and increased by 3   **(d)** ⁻7 and increased by 4
   (e) ⁺6 and decreased by 13   **(f)** ⁻5 and increased by 5?

4 How many units has the lever been moved when it changes from
   (a) ⁻3 to ⁺4   **(b)** ⁺6 to ⁻3   **(c)** ⁺7 to 0   **(d)** ⁻5 to ⁺3   **(e)** ⁺7 to ⁻4?

5 Karen Morris, Freddy's chief
   accountant, has the combination of the
   safe written down on paper. ⟨5↓⟩means
   turn the knob 5 places **clockwise** and
   ↓3⟩ means turn the knob 3 places **anti-
   clockwise**. What number will the
   arrow be pointing to when she opens
   the safe?

Challenge

Combination
Start at 7
↓5 , ↑1
↓6 , 3↓
↓4 , 2↓

Ask your teacher what to do next.

1 Name the shapes in each
tiling pattern like this:
A – isosceles triangles

A

B

C

D

E

F

G

H

I

2 Work as a group.

(a) Each cut out the four triangles from **Workbook page 22**.
Make a tiling pattern by sticking the triangles on a large
sheet of paper.

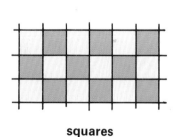

(b) Any four-sided shape can be called a quadrilateral.
Repeat part **(a)** for the quadrilaterals on **Workbook page 22**.

You can use any triangle or quadrilateral to make a tiling pattern.

Regular shapes have all their sides equal **and** all their angles equal.
Only some regular shapes make tiling patterns **on their own.**

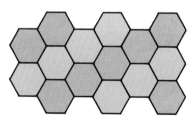

squares   equilateral triangles   regular hexagons

3 (a) Use a set of tiles or gummed shapes to make a tiling of **regular hexagons**.
(b) Do Workbook page 37, question 1.

4 Try to make a tiling of
(a) regular pentagons   **(b)** regular octagons.
Write about what happens.

5 Do Workbook page 37, questions 2 and 3, and Workbook page 38.

Work as a group.

1 (a) Each cut out the tiles from **Workbook page 20**.

(b) Fit the tiles together to make the three **different** patterns shown below.
Make **another** pattern with the tiles.

(c) Stick the tiles on a large sheet of paper to make the pattern you like best.

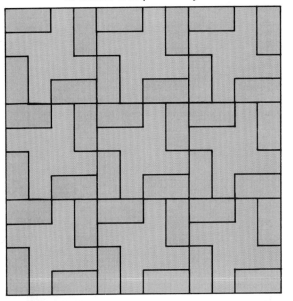

2 (a) Decide as a group how to colour the tiles at the foot of **Workbook page 26**. You could colour all of them the same . . .

or use different colours . . .

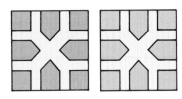

(b) Colour the tiles and cut them out.

(c) Experiment with different ways of fitting them together. Stick the tiles on a large sheet of paper to make a pattern.

3 (a) Repeat question **2** for the other sets of tiles on **Workbook page 26**.

(b) Design your own tiles on squared paper and make patterns with them.

Ask your teacher what to do next.

Work as a group.

1
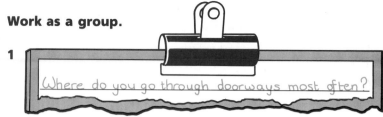
Where do you go through doorways most often?

To answer this question you might decide to collect data on an **observation sheet**.

Discuss which of these three observation sheets would be best. Write about why you think so.

Where do you go through
doorways most often?

Home ✓✓✓✓✓✓✓✓✓
School ✓✓✓✓✓✓✓✓✓✓✓✓✓
Elsewhere ✓✓✓✓

Where do you go through
doorways most often?
Name: Ann Black   Day: Friday

Every time you go through a
doorway write H if at home,
S if at school, E if elsewhere.

H H H H H E E S S S S S S S S S S
S S S E E S S S S S S S E E E E
H H H H

Where do you go through
doorways most often?
Name: John Rae   Day: Friday

Each time you go through a
doorway make a tally mark
in one of the sections.

Home: ⊬⊬⊬ ⊬⊬⊬ III
                              Total: 13

School: ⊬⊬⊬ ⊬⊬⊬ II
                              Total: 12

Elsewhere: ⊬⊬⊬ II
                              Total: 7

2

How many books, magazines and newspapers
do you look at during one day?

(a) Design an observation sheet for this question.
(b) Compare your group's observation sheet with one designed by another group.
Which is better? Write about why you think so.

3 (a) Each of you write as many words as you can in 2 minutes using some or all of these letters:
A C C E H I N N O P T

(b) Copy and complete this observation sheet for your words. ⟶

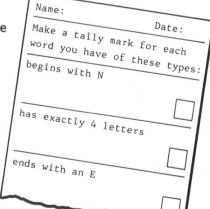
Name:
                    Date:
Make a tally mark for each
word you have of these types:

begins with N

has exactly 4 letters

ends with an E

4 (a) Each of you write as many names of boys and girls as you can in 2 minutes.
(b) Work as a group. Design an observation sheet to organise the data from this activity.
(c) Make copies of your observation sheet and give them to another group to complete.
(d) Was your observation sheet well designed? Write about why you think so.

1 Some pupils at Derwent School took part in a sponsored swim. The number of lengths completed by each swimmer is shown.

9	25	14	12	28	4	22	25
19	17	8	29	18	19	13	27
20	21	24	26	13	18	23	22

(a) How many pupils took part in the swim?
(b) Use your calculator.
Find • the total number of lengths completed
• the mean number of lengths completed.

2 What was **(a)** the lowest **(b)** the highest number of lengths completed?

The 'number of lengths completed' ranges from 4 to 29.
The **range** is 29−4=**25**. Because the range is large the numbers of lengths are grouped in **class intervals**.
In the table below, the size of the class interval is **five** as each includes five numbers. For example, the class interval 16–20 includes 16, 17, 18, 19 and 20.

3 (a) List the 'number of lengths' included in these class intervals:
• 11–15 • 26–30
(b) How many class intervals are there in the frequency table?
(c) Copy and complete the frequency table.
(d) **Go to Workbook page 42**, and show this information on Graph 1.

Number of lengths	Tally marks	Frequency
1 – 5		
6 – 10		
11 – 15		
16 – 20		
21 – 25		
26 – 30		
Total		

4 The record sheet shows the number of lengths completed by the teachers who took part in the swim.
(a) Copy and complete:
The number of lengths ranged
from _____ to _____.
The range is _____.
(b) Copy and complete the frequency table below.

**Sponsored swim Record Sheet
Lengths completed**

J. Adams	53	W. McCue	30
M. Ahmed	72	S. Mann	50
P. Bell	35	W. Martin	52
F. Carr	66	G. O'May	68
P. Cole	21	J. Orr	71
G. Doyle	85	D. Pascall	48
N. Faulds	38	A. Pilley	57
J. Geddes	69	J. Powers	53
W. Hall	72	A. Queen	69
J. Jackson	47	A. Rae	70
T. Kerr	43	D. Ramsay	51
R. Lockie	69	W. Rossl	66
J. McArthur	51	S. Taylor	44
P. McCall	55	W. Walker	25
R. McCaskill	60	I. Young	40

Number of lengths	Tally marks	Frequency
20 – 29		
30 – 39		
40 – 49		
50 – 59		
60 – 69		
70 – 79		
80 – 89		
Total		

(c) Go to **Workbook page 42** and show this information on Graph 2.

1 The 30 pupils in Class 1 at Derwent
School held a sponsored silence. The
length of time in minutes that each
pupil remained silent is shown.

Each bar graph uses a different size of
class interval to show the results of the
sponsored silence.

1	5	16	14	17	11
24	10	6	17	12	15
3	15	18	2	16	17
22	13	12	14	9	10
21	13	19	16	19	10

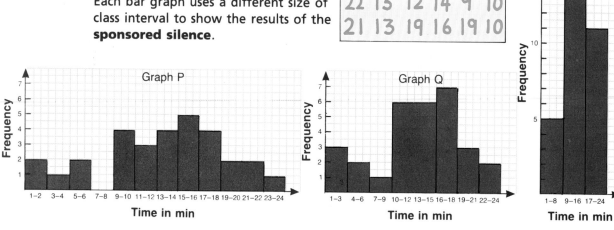

Graph P — Frequency vs Time in min

Graph Q — Frequency vs Time in min

Graph R — Frequency vs Time in min

(a) For each of the three graphs P, Q and R, give
  - the size of the class intervals
  - the number of class intervals.
(b) Which graph shows
  - most detail
  - least detail?
(c) **Do Workbook page 43. You will need the results of
the sponsored silence.**

2 List suitable class intervals
for each sponsored event
in the table. Try to have
from 5 to 12 intervals.

	Sponsored event		
	Silence	Spelling	Sums
Lowest result	1 minute	3 correct	24 correct
Highest result	48 minutes	69 correct	100 correct

3 Here are the results of a **sponsored sums** event. They show
the number of sums answered correctly by each pupil.

14	8	24	21	12	20	25	19	16	21
1	26	20	10	25	21	15	27	18	12
24	30	22	22	7	16	19	20	32	4

(a) Use the results to make a frequency table
with from 5 to 12 class intervals.
(b) Draw a bar graph.

4 Hold a sponsored event for
your class.
Collect data and draw a graph.

Some members of Parkhill Youth Club
took part in a fun run. The graph shows
the times to the nearest minute of the
boys who took part.

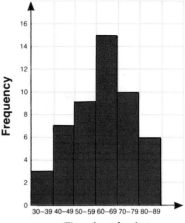

Time in minutes

1 (a) What is the size in minutes of each
class interval?
(b) How many class intervals are there?
(c) In which class interval are most
runners?
(d) How many boys took part in the
run?
(e) How many of the boys had a time
of less than 1 hour?

2 The times to the nearest minute of the
thirty **girls** who took part in the fun
run are shown opposite.
(a) Copy and complete:
The girls' times range from ____ min to ____ min.
The range is ____ min.

(b) Using the data, make and complete
a frequency table, choosing
suitable class intervals.
(c) Draw a graph using the
information from your table.

Parkhill Youth Club – Girls' times

62	86	44	52	81	93
50	71	69	81	78	75
67	88	81	61	79	85
78	71	94	86	75	75
97	79	63	92	75	89

3 Before the start of the run, some of
the members weighed themselves to
the nearest kilogram. Their weights are
shown opposite.
(a) Copy and complete:
The weights range from ____ kg to ____ kg.
The range is ____ kg.
(b) Using the data, make and complete
a frequency table.
(c) Draw a graph, using the
information from your table.

Parkhill Youth Club – Weights

67	63	56	49	52	61
73	59	53	57	51	59
54	57	56	49	59	50
58	64	58	54	56	58
66	55	66	52	57	64

Ask your teacher what to do next.

Gladeside School,
School Walk,
Ashdown.

11th January.

GLADESIDE SCHOOL

Dear Parent,

I propose to take a party of pupils for a study week to Invercarron Field Centre, near Kenby, from 27th May to 1st June. There will be walking, climbing, map reading, as well as outings of educational interest. Travel to the Centre will be by coach.

The inclusive cost of the field week will be £75 per pupil. Pupils wishing to go should give their names to me by the end of January along with a deposit of £15. The remainder of the cost must be paid by 24th May and can be paid weekly.

Full details of the field week will be given at a meeting to be held in the school on 23rd January at 7.30 p.m.

Yours sincerely,

D. W. Aitken

Headteacher.

INVERCARRON · FIELD CENTRE ·

January		February		March	
Sun	6 13 20 27		3 10 17 24		3 10 17 24 31
Mon	7 14 21 28		4 11 18 25		4 11 18 25
Tue	1 8 15 22 29		5 12 19 26		5 12 19 26
Wed	2 9 16 23 30		6 13 20 27		6 13 20 27
Thu	3 10 17 24 31		7 14 21 28		7 14 21 28
Fri	4 11 18 25		1 8 15 22		1 8 15 22 29
Sat	5 12 19 26		2 9 16 23		2 9 16 23 30

April		May		June	
Sun	7 14 21 28		5 12 19 20		2 9 16 23 30
Mon	1 8 15 22 29		6 13 20 27		3 10 17 24
Tue	2 9 16 23 30		7 14 21 28		4 11 18 25
Wed	3 10 17 24		1 8 15 22 29		5 12 19 26
Thu	4 11 18 25		2 9 16 23 30		6 13 20 27
Fri	5 12 19 26		3 10 17 24 31		7 14 21 28
Sat	6 13 20 27		4 11 18 25		1 8 15 22 29

July		August		September	
Sun	7 14 21 28		4 11 18 25		1 8 15 22 29
Mon	1 8 15 22 29		5 12 19 26		2 9 16 23 30
Tue	2 9 16 23 30		6 13 20 27		3 10 17 24

1 On what day of the week does the field week
   (a) start   (b) finish?

*2 (a) How many days does the field week last?
   (b) What is the average cost per day for each child?

3 After the date of the letter:
   (a) how many **schooldays** are there for names to be given to the headteacher
   (b) how many **complete weeks** are there until the start of the field week?

4 **You need this year's calendar.**
   Imagine that **this year** your headteacher sent out a letter similar to the one above. Which dates for this year correspond to the **five** dates given in the letter?

   Write these dates in a table like this.

Date in Gladeside school letter		Date this year
11th January ⟶	second Friday in January	⟶

Total cost of field week £75
Deposit paid £15
BALANCE to be paid ☐

5 (a) How much is the **balance** that each pupil still has to pay?

(b) Maureen decides to pay her balance in 15 weekly payments. How much will she pay per week?

(c) Brian pays his balance by making a payment of £5 each Friday, except for the first two Fridays in April when the school is on Easter holiday. If he makes his first payment on 15th February, on what date will he make his final payment?

6 Miss Wilkins collects the payments made by the pupils. One week 4 pupils each paid £6, 12 pupils each paid £5, and 9 pupils each paid £4.

(a) How many pupils made a payment in that week?

(b) How much money was paid to Miss Wilkins altogether?

(c) What was the **average** amount of money paid by each pupil?

7 (a) Draw this copy of the Gladeside badge on centimetre squared paper.

(b) What is the shape of the badge?

(c) Name **three** different shapes on the badge.

(d) Using **three** colours, colour your drawing of the badge so that it has *one* **line of symmetry**.

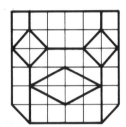

8 Work in a group.

On squared paper make a coloured enlargement of either the Gladeside badge or your own school badge, suitable for placing in a coach window.

9 The map shows different possible routes between the school and Invercarron Centre. The distances in kilometres between the road junctions ( ) are marked in red. How far is it between the school and the centre by

(a) the longest route **(b)** the shortest route?

10 The route taken by the school coach is 256 km long.

(a) Copy or trace the map and colour the route taken.

(b) If the coach takes 4 hours for the journey, what is its average speed in kilometres per hour?

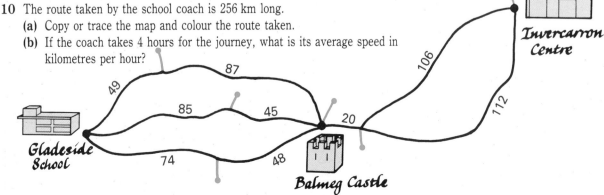

Ben Carron 1250m

King's Se
1195m

1090m Eagle Cliffs

Chair Lif
650m

4 · · · 725m

3½

Windy Ridge

1

3½

6½

2

Loch Carron

350m
Campsite

3½

The Hills

1 Look at the view shown above from Invercarron Field Centre. White Cairn is 1220 metres high. Write the names of the three highest hills in order, starting with the highest.

2 How much higher is Ben Carron than **(a)** King's Seat **(b)** Black Craig?

3 Find the difference in height between the campsite and
 (a) the chair lift **(b)** the top of Ben Carron
 (c) Eagle Cliffs **(d)** Windy Ridge.

The Walks

4 The distances in kilometres between places are shown by the red numbers. What is the distance from the campsite to **(a)** Windy Ridge **(b)** the chair lift?

The pupils from Gladeside School plan walks to explore the countryside. They expect to take 15 minutes for each kilometre they walk.

5 How long should they allow for these walks in the spruce forest:
 (a) the red trail **(b)** the yellow trail **(c)** the blue trail?

6 A notice board shows the walking times from Invercarron to some other places. Calculate the distance in kilometres to each place.

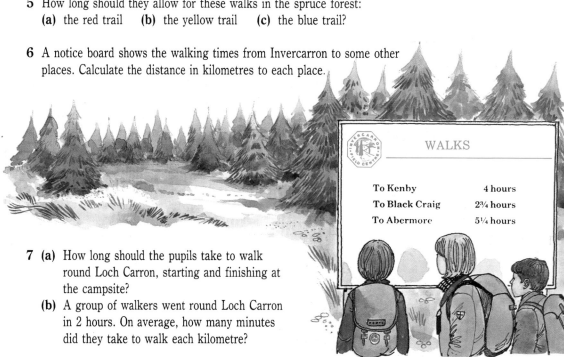

WALKS

To Kenby	4 hours
To Black Craig	2¾ hours
To Abermore	5¼ hours

7 **(a)** How long should the pupils take to walk round Loch Carron, starting and finishing at the campsite?
 (b) A group of walkers went round Loch Carron in 2 hours. On average, how many minutes did they take to walk each kilometre?

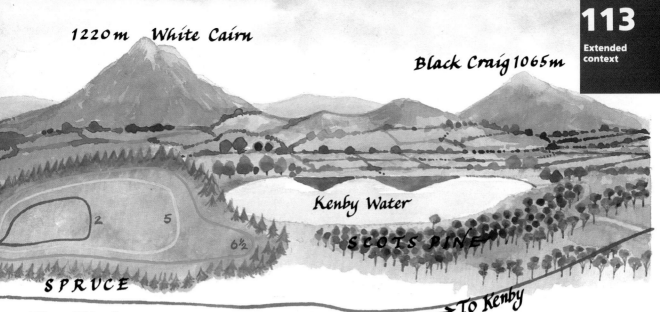

The Climbs

When planning a walk onto the hills Maureen's group expects to take

- 15 minutes for each kilometre walked

and, **in addition**

- 1 hour for each 300 metres climbed.

8 What total time should they allow for these hillwalks, starting from the campsite
   (a) to the chair lift **(b)** by way of Windy Ridge to the top of Ben Carron?

9 **(a)** What total time should they allow for this hillwalk?

   Start at the campsite, go by way of Windy Ridge to the top of Ben Carron and return by the same route to the campsite.

   (b) Describe a different route they could take for the Ben Carron hillwalk, starting and finishing at the campsite.

   (c) How long should they allow for this hillwalk?

   (d) If the group sets out on this hillwalk at 9.30 am, about what time would you expect them to return?

The Forests

10 This graph shows the areas of ground covered by different kinds of trees at the Invercarron Centre.

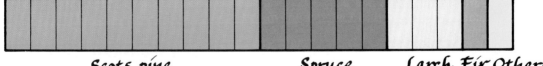

Scots pine   Spruce   Larch Fir Others

   (a) What fraction of this total area is covered by each kind of tree?
   (b) Give each fraction in **(a)** as a percentage.
   (c) The total area covered by trees is 1200 hectares. What area is covered by spruce trees?

11 Gary's group tried to estimate the number of trees in the spruce forest. They marked out an area of 100m^2 in the forest as shown and counted the trees in the area.

   (a) How many trees were there in the area of 100 m^2?
   (b) Write about how this information could be used to estimate the number of trees in the spruce forest.
   (c) About how many trees are there in the spruce forest?

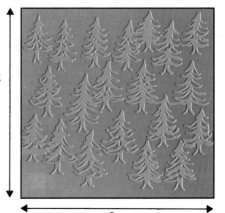

10 m

10 m

White Cairn

INVERCARRON FIELD CENTRE

The Gladeside party travelled by mini-bus from the centre to the chair lift.

The mini-bus carries up to 16 passengers.
It takes 3 minutes to load and 2 minutes to unload the mini-bus.
The journey took 15 minutes to the chair lift and 10 minutes back to the centre.

1 How many journeys were needed to transport the party of 26 pupils and 4 teachers to the chair lift?

2 The first group started to load the mini-bus at 09.30. At what time
   (a) was the first group unloaded at the chair lift
   (b) did the mini-bus arrive back at the centre
   (c) was the whole party unloaded at the chair lift
   (d) did the empty mini-bus return again to the centre?

3 What was the latest time the mini-bus could have left the centre to bring the **whole party** back by 16.00?

Chair Lift Information

Speed of chairs	2 metres per second
Length of lower section	600 m
Length of upper section	

4 (a) How many minutes does it take to travel from the bottom to the top of the **lower** section of the chair lift?
   (b) The chair lift information sign is damaged. Calculate the length of the **upper** section if it takes 8 minutes to travel from the bottom of it to the top.

5 A chair holds two people. Empty chairs pass the pick-up point every 10 seconds. How long will it take for all 26 pupils and 4 teachers to get on to the chair lift?

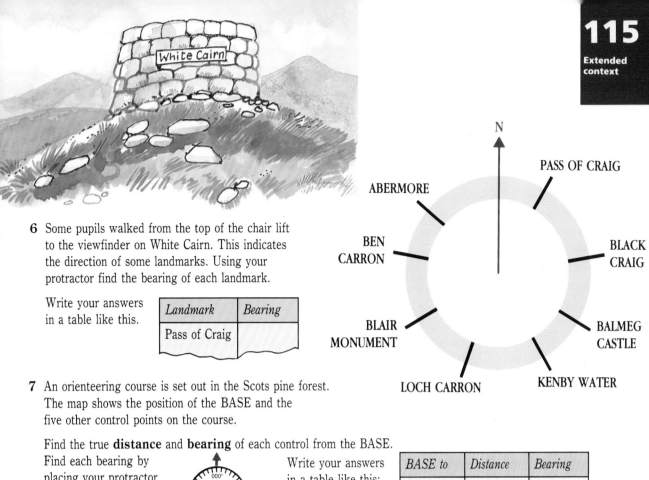

6 Some pupils walked from the top of the chair lift to the viewfinder on White Cairn. This indicates the direction of some landmarks. Using your protractor find the bearing of each landmark.

Write your answers in a table like this.

Landmark	Bearing
Pass of Craig	

7 An orienteering course is set out in the Scots pine forest. The map shows the position of the BASE and the five other control points on the course.

Find the true **distance** and **bearing** of each control from the BASE.

Find each bearing by placing your protractor on the BASE like this:

Write your answers in a table like this:

BASE to	Distance	Bearing
EAGLE	150 m	

Scale 1 cm to 30 m

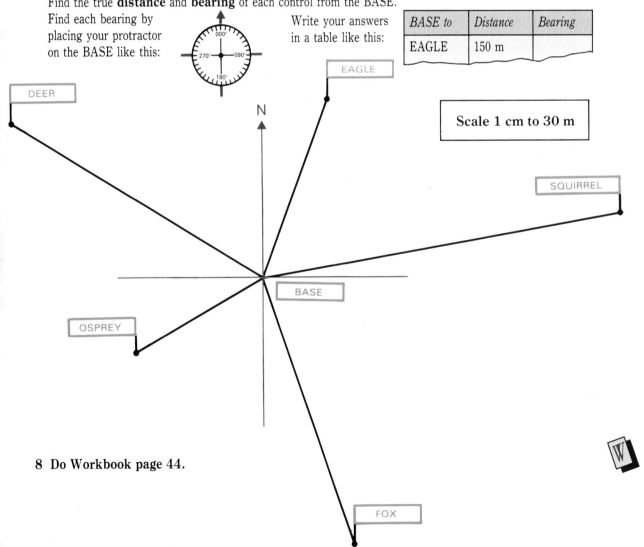

8 Do Workbook page 44.

KENBY

One afternoon the pupils from Gladeside School visited the nearby village of Kenby.
The map shows some places in and around Kenby.

1 Which places have co-ordinates **(a)** (5, 3)   **(b)** (4, 1)   **(c)** (1, 4)   **(d)** (6, 3)?

2 What are the co-ordinates of   **(a)** the motel   **(b)** the square
  (c) the golf clubhouse   **(d)** the hall?

3 What are the co-ordinates of each of the three places where a road crosses the river?

4 **(a)** Measure in centimetres the length of the line showing the scale of the map.
  (b) Copy and complete: __ cm represents 1 km, so 1 cm represents __ m

5 What is the true length of the **straight** road from the centre of the square
  to the point where it meets the path to the farmhouse?

6 **You need string or thread.**
  Brian and some of his friends walked from the square along the road to the
  motel and then followed the path of Kenby Water. They continued along the
  riverside to the road and then back to the square. How far did they walk
  altogether?

7 **Look carefully at the direction of North.**
  Which place is **(a)** due North of the square   **(b)** due West of the square
      (c) due East of the dry ski slope   **(d)** North East of the Hall?

8 In which direction is **(a)** the hall from the school   **(b)** the school from the church
      (c) the farmhouse from the school   **(d)** the golf clubhouse from the church?

One wet evening at Invercarron everyone from Gladeside stayed indoors. There was no TV at the centre so they made up some indoor activities. You can try some of them:

A wet evening

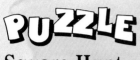

Square Hunt

There are **ten** squares in this pattern.

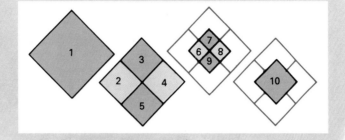

Use the patterns on **Workbook page 45** to help you find how many squares there are in this pattern. Colour, in separate patterns, each square that you find.

Triangle Hunt

Use the patterns on **Workbook page 45** to help you find how many **equilateral** triangles there are in this pattern. Colour each equilateral triangle that you find. You will need to colour several triangles in some of the patterns.

Making Squares

Use the dotty grids on **Workbook page 45**.

Rules
- Start at any dot.
- Without lifting your pencil from the paper, join dots using horizontal and vertical lines only.
- You **can** pass through the same dot more than once.
- You **cannot** join the same two dots more than once.

Scoring
- Score 4 for each complete square.
- Score 3 for a square with one side missing.
- Score 2 for a square with two sides missing.

Aim for as high a score as possible by drawing as many squares as you can.

The black numbers show one possible route.
The red numbers show the score – total 33.

The Gladeside Quiz

The quiz is on page 118. It was also given to some of the visitors who came to the school's open night after the school party returned from Invercarron.

Open night at Gladeside

After the school party returned to
Gladeside School they decided to have an
open night to tell everyone about their field
week at Invercarron.
Try some of their activities.

squirrel

fox

eagle

trout

1 Make an enlargement for a wall
display of one of these pictures
of wildlife seen at Invercarron.

2 Write about some of the things
the pupils did at Invercarron
in which they used mathematics.

3 Make a model of the
Invercarron centre.

4 Some visitors tried the **Gladeside Quiz**.

(a) There is a log 6 metres long in the Scots pine forest. A forester wishes
to cut it into six pieces each one metre long.
How long will it take him to do this if each cut takes him 1 minute?

(b) The Gladeside boys leave the campsite to walk round Loch Carron at an
average speed of 4 km per hour. The girls leave the campsite at the
same time to walk round the loch in the opposite direction. The girls
walk at an average speed of 4½ km per hour. When the two groups
meet which one will be nearer the campsite?

(c) Eight pupils throw eight stones into Loch Carron in eight seconds. How
long will it take three pupils to throw three stones into the loch?

(d) Copy this row of letters. Score out **seven letters** so that the remaining
letters, in order, form the name of a well-known place.

S I E N V V E E N R L C E A T R T R E O R N S

Some pages from the

Catalogue

Netball Game

◄ FOOTBALL
SE 6901
£13·35
20 weeks
at 67p

NETBALL GAME ►
SE 6902 **£15·99**
20 weeks
at 80p

RUGBY
BALL ►
SE 6904
£12·16
20 weeks
at 61p

◄ BOOTED
SKATES
SE 6907
£18·99
20 weeks
at 95p

◄ TWISTBALL
SE 6903
£12·90
20 weeks
at 65p

ICE SKATES
SE 6905
£29·99
20 weeks
at £1·50

◄ TENNIS SET
SE 6908
£12·95
20 weeks
at 65p

BADMINTON SET ►
SE 6906 **£25·99**
20 weeks
at £1·30

TABLE TENNIS SET
SE 6935 **£17·85**
20 weeks at 90p

SNOOKER TABLES
SE 6912 **£59·99**
20 weeks at £3
38 weeks at £1·60
SE 6913 **£39·99**
20 weeks at £2
38 weeks at £1·06

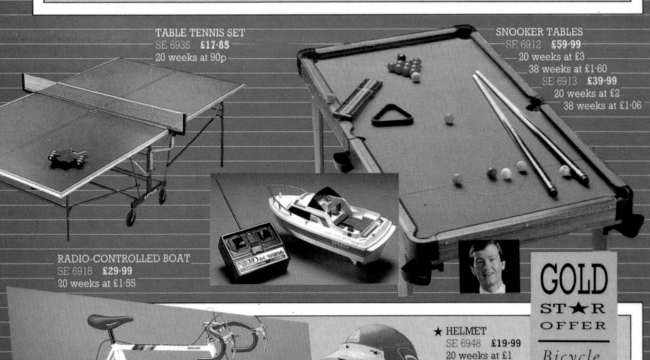

RADIO-CONTROLLED BOAT
SE 6918 **£29·99**
20 weeks at £1·55

★ HELMET
SE 6948 **£19·99**
20 weeks at £1

★ LIGHTING SET
SE 6947 **£7·99**
20 weeks at 40p

★ BICYCLE
SE 6946 **£89·90**
20 weeks at £4·50
38 weeks at £2·40
50 weeks at £1·85

JACKET *80% wool 20% cotton*

Heights: 128, 134, 140, 146, 152, 158 cm

	CC 1518	**£24·99**

T-SHIRT *cotton*

Chest:			
61/63 cm	CC 1642	**£6·50**
66/69 cm	CC 1643	**£6·99**
71/74 cm	CC 1644	**£7·50**
76/78 cm	CC 1645	**£7·99**

JEANS *cotton*

Waist:			
51, 54 cm	CC 1321	**£14·99**
56, 58 cm	CC 1322	**£15·99**
61, 63 cm	CC 1323	**£16·49**
66, 69 cm	CC 1324	**£17·49**

Each item in
White, pink or navy

SWEATSHIRT *cotton*

Height: 122/128 cm		
	CC 1420	**£12·99**
Height: 134/140 cm		
	CC 1421	**£13·99**
Height: 146/152, 158 cm		
	CC 1422	**£14·99**

RED BLUE GREEN
YELLOW ORANGE

Flying suit

canvas
YELLOW RED BLUE

Heights: 134, 140, 146, 152, 158 cm
CC 1296 **£26·99**

STRIPED T-SHIRT *50% cotton 50% polyester*

WHITE/RED   WHITE/BLUE
WHITE/GREEN   WHITE/YELLOW

Chest: 61, 63, 66, 69, 71 cm		
	CC 1681	**£6·50**
74, 76, 78, 81 cm		
	CC 1684	**£6·99**

GIRLS OR BOYS

JOGGING

DENIM JACKET
cotton

Chest:		
61, 63, 66, 69, 71 cm		
CC 1570 GREY		
CC 1567 BLUE	**£19·99**
Chest:		
74, 76, 78, 81 cm		
CC 1571 GREY		
CC 1568 BLUE	**£22·50**

SWEATSHIRT

50% cotton   50% acrylic

WHITE BLUE RED

Chest: 61/63, 66/69 cm		
	CC 1467	**£7·99**
Chest: 71/76, 78/84 cm		
	CC 1470	**£8·99**

JOG JACKET
(various colours)

50% cotton   50% acrylic

Height: 128/134 cm		
	CC 1547	**£12·99**
Height: 140/146 cm		
152/158 cm		
	CC 1549	**£14·49**

JOG TROUSERS
(various colours)

Waist: 58/61 cm		
63/66 cm		
	CC 1380	**£11·99**
Waist: 69/71 cm		
74/76 cm		
	CC 1382	**£12·99**

BOY'S JEANS *cotton*

WHITE BLUE GREY
RED BROWN

Waist: 61, 63, 66 cm		
	CC 1390	**£12·99**
Waist: 69, 71, 74 cm		
	CC 1391	**£14·99**

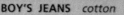

Goodies

COLOUR TRIM
BLUE PINK

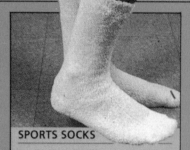

COLOUR TRIM
GREY RED BLUE

SPORTS SHOES

for all indoor sports

Sizes 11, 12, 13, 1, 2	FW 7107	£11·99
Sizes 3, 4, 5, 6	FW 7108	£12·99

ANKLE BOOTS

Sizes: 11, 12, 13, 1, 2	FW 7101	£6·99
Sizes 3, 4, 5, 6	FW 7102	£7·99

Heights:

122/128 cm	SW 7121	£18·11
134/140 cm	SW 7122	£18·48
146/152 cm	SW 7123	£19·65
158/164 cm	SW 7124	£20·23

TRAINERS

Sizes: 11, 12, 13, 1, 2 GREY FW 7103 BLACK FW 7104		£10·99
Sizes 3, 4, 5, 6 GREY FW 7105 BLACK FW 7106		£11·99

SPORTS SOCKS

Sizes: To fit shoe 11–2 WHITE SW 7113 BLUE SW 7114		£1·39
To fit shoe 3–6 WHITE SW 7115 BLUE SW 7116		£1·59

SPORTS SHIRTS

Chest: 61/63, 66/69 cm	RED SW 7109	WHITE SW 7110		£7·49
Chest: 71/76, 78/84 cm	RED SW 7111	WHITE SW 7112		£8·99

SPORTS SHORTS

Waist: 56, 61, 66 cm	NAVY BLUE SW 7117	WHITE SW 7118		£4·89
Waist: 71, 76 cm	NAVY BLUE SW 7119	WHITE SW 7120		£5·75

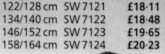

BOYS & GIRLS VARIOUS COLOURS

TRACKSUITS

Bebo

SUPERB BUY

EG 7201
COLOUR TV with TELETEXT
20 weeks at £26 per week
38 weeks at £15

£520

VHS VIDEOTAPES
EG 7210   3 tapes for £7·10

Scotch
Scotch

£460

VHS EDLER VIDEO RECORDER
EG 7203
20 weeks at £23   38 weeks at £13

Credi

£125

RADIO CASSETTE RECORDER
EG 7202
20 weeks at £6·30 per week

Personal stereos

BISH HS EG 7212
20 weeks at £4·50

BUBI KT EG 7211
20 weeks at £2

£90

£294

£39·95

DEAHA LT   20 weeks at £15
EG 7213   38 weeks at £8

Buy a video of your favourite Pop group.
Any one tape → £10
EG 7204 THE MOVERS
EG 7205 PEACH
EG 7206 SHOOTING STARS
EG 7207 BELAMAY

FREE POSTER
if you order 2 videos

THE MOVERS
BELAMAY
Shooting Stars
PEACH

Pop videos

Cameras

£430

SPECIAL OFFER →

EG 7208
SCOTT BILBERRY –
GREATEST
HITS £6·99

VIDEO CAMERA
EG 7209
20 weeks at £22 per week
38 weeks at £13 per week

£38·90

Tika

on this VETA kit
EG 7216
was £149
now £129

SAVE £20

20 weeks at £6·60
38 weeks at £3·50

BARGAIN

£18·90

LINOX CAMERA
Fits in your pocket
EG 7217

Self-focussing
EG 7218

Films   35 mm colour

Lota

24 exposures EG 7220 £2·25
36 exposures EG 7221 £2·80

DEVELOPING

£2·99 EG 7222
£3·59 EG 7223

Kodacolor
Gold
Kodak

SUPER CALCULATOR
Solar powered
EG 7219

SPECIAL OFFER

Records

We have the top twenty albums
Any LP £4·50 EG 7214

EURYTHMICS

So

£6·60

SPECIAL BUY

Number 1 album
EG 7215 always £4

Goodies

PERSONAL GIFTS

POSTERS

PG 392 Two horses

PG 391 Concorde

SMALL	95p
60 cm × 40 cm	
LARGE	£2·20
90 cm × 60 cm	

PG 390 Rocket

PG 393 Tiger

PG 394 Pop group

PG 395 Rock festival

NAME pendants

☆ 9ct GOLD PG 386 £38
☆ Up to 10 letters
☆ Your name, a friend's name, favourite pop star, football team. . . .
☆ Also in silver PG385 £24

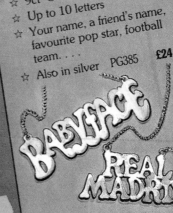

SPECIAL offer
Set of six, all different

LARGE PG 400 £9
SMALL PG 399 £5

FOR YOUR DOOR . . .

NAME PLATES
PG 402
15 cm × 6 cm
£2·48

Janine

SPECIAL NOTICES

PG 401

BUSY FEEDING CROCODILE
but come in anyway

Cost per letter:
Gold **10p**
Silver **9p**
Black **7p**

STICKERS

	SMALL packet of 8		32p
	GIANT pack of 100		£3
	SUPERGIANT pack of 250		£7

	SMALL	GIANT	SUPERGIANT PG 490
	PG 471	PG 485	PG 491
Pop stars	PG 472	PG 486	PG 492
Sporting heroes	PG 473	PG 487	PG 493
Dogs	PG 474	PG 488	
Film stars			

SPECIAL OFFER ALBUM for stickers **£8** (holds 500) PG 499

☆ Sensational **T-SHIRTS** with your own message!

NEW

T-shirts without messages

	Red	White	Blue	
			PG 433	£4
LARGE	PG 431	PG 432	PG 436	£3·49
MEDIUM	PG 434	PG 435	PG 439	£2·99
SMALL	PG 437	PG 438		

Messages: LARGE PRINT **17p** per letter (maximum 15 letters)
SMALL PRINT **13p** per letter (maximum 30 letters)

ANY MESSAGE BADGES FREE

LARGE **72p** PG 407

SMALL **36p** PG 408

MATHS IS MAGIC

---

with your OWN NAME

TOOTHBRUSH
64p PG 494

ADD 2p PER LETTER FOR NAME

PENCILS PACK OF 10
£1·30 PG 495

ADD 3p PER LETTER FOR NAME

RULER
25 cm **40p** PG 496
20 cm **32p** PG 497

ADD 1p PER LETTER FOR NAME